Dream Interpretation

Is God's Business

BRENT MASSEY

Massey, Brent.
    Dream Interpretation / Brent Massey.
    p. cm.
    1. Christianity 2. Dream interpretation 3. Holy Spirit I. Title.
    ISBN 0-9790397-5-4

Printed in the USA, UK and around the world.

The cover photo is public domain. It is a 19th-century painting by Adrien Guignet depicting Joseph explaining Pharaoh's dream.

"Interpreting dreams is
God's business"
(Genesis 40:8 NLT).

DEDICATION

This is dedicated to the Lord and my family.

ALSO BY BRENT MASSEY

Culture Shock! Hawai'i

Where in the World Do I Belong??

Discovering the Water of Life

Contents

Preface: As I Grow

There is a gift of faith in my family heritage. Both of my great-grandfathers on my mother's side were preachers, Baptist and Methodist. My great-great-grandfather was a circuit-riding Methodist preacher who planted the first Methodist church in Chico, Texas. On my father's side, my great-grandfather has his name on a plaque in the sanctuary of the Methodist Church in Comanche, Oklahoma.

When I was around nine years old my mother and I visited a Bible study on the east coast, and a black lady pastor with a gift of prophecy prayed over me and said I had a gift of faith and would share it with many people. Some time after that my mother had a dream of me speaking or preaching about my faith to a stadium or big auditorium of people.

Later, when I was in junior high, the youth pastor who prayed with me to accept Christ, told my mother I had a gift of faith and would be using it to speak to large groups of people. A few years ago, I told my mother that her dream could have been symbolic of my blog at the time, which had about forty thousand total visitors, but it could also be about this dream book and/or ministry.

I was motivated to write this book because over the years I've had many dreams that God used to guide me and even show me what was to come. However, I wasn't finding any support in the church and very little resources to better understand how the Lord was using my dreams to speak to me.

One person commented on my blog: "I agree that you are right that there is not enough teaching on dreams, when quite clearly the Bible has condoned dream interpretation as normal. Do you think that dreams can be used as a form of warning? As this could come under what you described as a prognostic or prophetic dream...and then what are the point of these dreams—just to have discernment into what is happening, or to use wisdom and act accordingly? This then could be taken to the level where you are running around a bit fruity-like, reacting to things. It didn't seem Joseph acted because of his dreams, except in the case where he advised the king to fill the storehouse in preparation for the famine... Ahhh. Funny, I think I might have just answered my own Q. Thanks again for the posts!"

Another person commented, "I especially agree with the church not tending to God speaking through dreams. God speaks to me through dreams regularly, and yet I never hear about that in large church settings—only in personal conversation. I think it should be emphasized. I felt as if I was

God speaks to me through dreams regularly, and yet I never hear about that in large church settings.

alone in His speaking that way until I spoke more with other Christians and realized that it's common, just not spoken enough about."

Another person commented, "Others seem to think that because they don't have this happen in their lives that we are making it up or are delusional."

Insight into ourselves

Herman Riffel, a long-time Baptist minister and author of *Dream Interpretation: A Biblical Understanding*, said the uninterpreted dream is like an unopened letter. God uses dreams to communicate with us. He guides us, warns us, and shows us the parts of our lives that we need to examine or surrender. Sometimes our dreams are God's way of bringing us to our knees through nightmares and yelling in our sleep. Riffel says that people in crisis (which may also include many defeated Christians) frequently are interested in understanding what God is trying to tell them through their dreams.

I have had dreams that warn me, like whether my ego and pride is out of control, or my anger is a danger for that day. I will wait and see how the day unfolds and watch for the situation where I need to exercise caution. Sometimes I will think it's one situation, but then later in the day it's actually another because the symbols, details and feelings in the dream line up with what is happening at that moment. Then, I am proactive to be careful to heed the warning from the Lord that came through my dream.

How I Interpret

I still don't know whether God speaks to us through every dream, and like many people I have lots of dreams, so I trust His leading in deciding which dreams I try to understand, journal and write about. Many times I journal and try to interpret the ones that stand out to me, strike my interest, or have intense feelings in them.

How I do dream interpretation is fairly simple. First I pray and ask the Lord to help me remember and understand my dream, remembering it's only important if He is trying to speak to me through it. Maybe once a week I end up journaling a day or two of dreams that I think I should record. I have to spend a hour or more just writing out dream(s) when I have them. I want to catch everything because any detail can have some significance that adds to understanding the whole. Other dreams I just try to keep in mind for a few days to see if anything pops up.

My dreams seem to come in waves with more frequency during hard times. There are periods when I have occasional dreams, and they never seem to amount to anything. Whereas, when I was going through battles at church and in between jobs, He showed me at least weekly if not more often something that was going to happen that day or week. One person commented, "He must keep a steady stream of communication going with you. Mine is more intermittent."

Feelings are a great tool for indicating what the dream is about. I ask myself, "Where in my waking life have I been experiencing the same feelings I had in my dream?" I also keep all the symbols in mind that occurred in my dream to see if He will show me later what they mean, like He did with my Answers in Genesis dream. One person commented on my blog, "I don't know what mine mean sometimes until they are upon me." I have to agree. Many times I have a notion about what the Lord is telling me, but other times I don't know what my dreams are about until it smacks me in the face, and I'm right in the midst of them or after the fact.

One person commented, "We absolutely must pray for discernment to interpret our dreams. Dream dictionaries are too generalized to be accurate. God's interaction with us individually is unique and must be understood in this context. Just as parents teach their children in different ways according to their ability to comprehend, knowing just how to reach that child, so our Heavenly Father speaks to us."

Lastly, this book is a culmination of many years of Bible study, and research, writing, and journaling about dreams. In my last book, *Discovering the Water of Life* (2008), I had a section on Christian dream interpretation, which included many Jungian concepts such as darkside, masculine/ feminine, unconscious, psyche, etc. Since my last book, I have completely dropped any form of Jungian dream interpretation. God reveals the meaning of our dreams to us, and it's not through man's wisdom, and using Jungian concepts is like the astrologers who invented interpretations of Nebuchadnezzar's dreams.

"Daniel answered the king and said, "No wise men, enchanters, magicians, or astrologers can show to the king the mystery that the king has asked, but there is a God in heaven who reveals mysteries, and He has made known to King Nebuchadnezzar what will be in the latter days" (Daniel 2:27-28).

1

Truth

Dream interpretation requires an ability and willingness to discern the truth. "You cannot observe your dreams and remain a phony Christian for long. Dreams will reveal what you are doing and will not allow you to ignore it." (*Dream Interpretation: A Biblical Understanding* by Herman Riffel).

Joseph shared dreams of his mother, father and brothers bowing down to him, but his family couldn't handle the truth. Joseph's father berated him, and his brothers eventually retaliated by selling him into slavery in Egypt.

> "Joseph had a dream, and when he told it to his brothers, they hated him all the more. He said to them, "Listen to this dream I had: We were binding sheaves of grain out in the field when suddenly my sheaf rose and stood upright, while your sheaves gathered around mine and bowed down to it."
>
> His brothers said to him, "Do you intend to reign over us? Will you actually rule us?" And they hated him all the more because of his dream and what he had said.

Then he had another dream, and he told it to his brothers. "Listen," he said, "I had another dream, and this time the sun and moon and eleven stars were bowing down to me."
When he told his father as well as his brothers, his father rebuked him and said, "What is this dream you had? Will your mother and I and your brothers actually come and bow down to the ground before you?" His brothers were jealous of him, but his father kept the matter in mind" (Genesis 37:3-10).

Animal Instinct Dream

God has several times revealed the truth about my circumstances through my dreams. I once had a dream where the Lord revealed the works of my boss, co-worker, and a friend:

In my dream, there was a lion trying to get in the house, but it couldn't get in. Inside the house there was a hyena that I hit with a pole but didn't have effect. And at the front door, there was a gorilla that I tried to scare or push, but it was rigid and unmoved.

The Lord was showing me the characters and behaviors of the people in my workplace through the symbols of animals in my dream. The Holy Spirit doesn't lead non-Christians, so they act on their instincts instead—much like animals.

The lion represents aggression and ruling, trying to control people or situations and being in charge. "Be alert and of sober mind. Your enemy the devil prowls around like a roaring lion looking for someone to devour" (1 Peter 5:8).

The lion symbolized my boss who was frequently looking for ways to attack, but through the Lord's protection didn't succeed—thus couldn't get in the house.

According to an online dream dictionary, the hyena represents "laughter or taunting, danger, criticism or biting comments (due to hyenas' very strong jaws). They probably depict an attitude of living on other people's vulnerability or weakness; taking advantage of someone or being taken advantage of and underhandedness." It was surprising how well this description fit my coworker's behavior—even her hyena laugh was heard all the way down the hall. The Lord was also showing me that attacking her (to try to protect myself and keep her away) wouldn't have any effect.

The gorilla symbolizes "companionship, community; brute force, or possibly gentle strength. Dreaming of this gentle, kindhearted animal almost always signifies a new friendship, or the reaffirming of an old friendship."

One of my superiors, who is a friend, also looks very much like a friendly gorilla. He made some attacking comments but the Lord, through this dream, was showing me his gentle character and that I don't have to fear—instead just keep it as a friendly argument.

In my dream, I tried to scare or push the gorilla but to no effect; he was still rigid and unmoved. I've tried to convince him several times of his need for Jesus but he is unmoved to faith like Agrippa II, in Acts 26, who said, "do you think you can make a Christian so quickly?"

One person commented, "It's very frightening that the devil stalks us like a lion! May we all wear the armor of God for protection at all times!"

"I think that many women are like the hyena of your dream. Your description fits my sister—biting comments, criticism, underhandedness. It's interesting that in your dream you hit the hyena with a pole which had no effect at all on the hyena.

The song that kept playing in my mind was in reference to my sister: Lay down, lay down,

> Lay your sword down,
>
> For the way of the Lord
>
> Is truth and life.

I initially did lay down my sword, but when she attacked me for the second time, I drew my sword like a warrior. But, like you, my physical weapon had no effect. It is futile to try and fight a human battle with a 'hyena-like spirit'. We can only counter it with truth. My solution has been total avoidance and trying to counter all her lies with truth."

Prophecy and Truth

Some American Christians (even pastors) frown on people who say they heard from God—especially if it was in a dream. In the Bible, there are plenty of examples of people hearing from God through their dreams. There are also many examples of people hearing from God, but it doesn't mention how they heard from Him. I believe that in many of these cases they were hearing from God through their dreams because hearing from God through their dreams was an accepted part of their culture.

In the American church, there is a misunderstanding about the spiritual gift of prophecy—many people imagine it's like fortune telling. According to the Life Application Study Bible, "Prophecy is not a sermon, but a spontaneous, Spirit-inspired message that is orally delivered in the congregation for the edification and encouragement of the Body of Christ. The ability to prophesy may involve predicting future events, but its main purpose is to communicate God's message to people, providing insight, warning, correction, and encouragement." Many times in the Bible prophecy took the form of written letters, so it's not limited to an orally delivered message. In the Bible, prophets were often the only people willing to speak the truth into a situation.

Some Americans aren't afraid to confront, attack, or even sue their neighbor—if they feel their rights have been violated—but most Americans are unwilling and afraid to speak the truth to their neighbor about their unchristian behavior or defects in character. Some people just plain don't care, others are afraid of being called a hypocrite, condemning, judging, or self-righteous. They are fearful, if they point out someone else's sin, they will have to look at their own sin. However, it's not showing love to let someone continue in their sin. Silence is a form of approval.

One Irish guy, who has traveled the world and lived in America, commented on his blog, "I wonder if political

There's way too much euphemism to avoid the hard truth.

correctness is in your constitution...there's way too much euphemism to avoid the hard truth. A lot of Americans I met feel very lonely, and I feel this is a major reason. You may never find a boy/girlfriend if a friend who knows you well and supposedly cares about you, doesn't tell you the hard facts of what makes you so damn annoying... so that you can change it! Being insulting for the sake of it is needless aggression. But constructive criticism is what friends are for."

Many times in the Bible people called Jesus a prophet—and He was the greatest Prophet—as well as the Son of God. As a prophet Jesus made many prophecies but also confronted the religious leaders of the day for many things—like their failure to understand the scriptures, their failure to love others, placing their own rules above God's commands, etc. The gift of prophecy involves not only foretelling events, but also speaking the truth in love.

The nature of the prophet hasn't changed, Paul used the same Greek word for Old Testament prophets as he did for New Testament ones. According to the Blue Letter Bible, this word was used "of men filled with the Spirit of God, who by God's authority and command in words of weight pleads the cause of God and urges salvation of men...in the religious assemblies of the Christians, they were moved by the Holy Spirit to speak, having power to instruct, comfort, encourage, rebuke, convict, and stimulate their hearers."

But if an unbeliever or an inquirer comes in while everyone is prophesying, they are convicted of sin and are brought under judgment by all, (1 Cor. 14:24).

Voice of Truth

When I was in grade school I attended a vacation Bible school and learned about the devil. At the time my mother, who was a Christian, didn't believe there was a devil. I came home and told her I believed there was a devil, and that spoke to her somehow, and shortly she came to realize the truth of it. A few years ago my mother told me she thinks I have the spiritual gift of prophecy "to call people to repentance in love". It's probably no surprise that one of my favorite movies is about the prophet Jeremiah, and one of my favorite songs is the Voice of Truth by Casting Crowns.

I know one logical minded fellow who gets ruffled when others are illogical or not factual. I have been told one of my qualities is that I am honest. I get ruffled when people fail to see or reject the truth. Pilate said to Jesus, "What is the truth?" Implying that there are many perspectives on that subject—but in the case of the Word of God there is only one truth despite peoples' efforts to twist it.

This is my fourth book, and there is common theme among all my books of trying to get the truth out there. In my first book I am exposing the fact that the culture of Hawaii is very different from mainland USA, and whites aren't necessarily at the top of the pecking order. In my second book I demonstrate how cultures around the world have very different preferences and reward different behaviors from American culture. In my third book I explain how I came into the truth of a living, loving, surrendered relationship with the Lord. The thrust of this book is to dispel the myths about prophecy and counter the lack of teaching regarding dream interpretation—in essence, get the truth out about prophecy and dreams.

Insight and Truth Dream

In 2012, I took a Biblical Studies class, and I was reading the textbook and thinking that it was poorly written because it had little insight and was filled with academic mumbo jumbo. I wondered if I could make it through the class with all the pressure I was already under at work and home. I started to stuff my face with cookies when I thought about all the papers and homework I had to get done for class that day.

After a couple hours, I picked up the assignment list and started to read through it, and then I looked in the book, went upstairs and started to write. The first paper on cultural norms just flowed out, and I went downstairs and told my wife how mentally refreshed I felt. I felt younger and recalled something about my youth (which I can't remember now). I hadn't blogged in probably a year (after I took down my website), and the last time I wrote anything was in a Bible class I took six months before.

I went back upstairs and wrote another paper and when I came downstairs, my wife told me that she and my sons had already been on a bike ride and played at the park. I had no idea that they had left. It was like when I used to write my books and blogs—the time had just slipped away effortlessly, and I didn't notice my surroundings.

I had a sort of PTSD around people and general jumpiness at work, but when I was writing none of that edginess or sensitivity was there. For a couple years I had to sleep alone without my wife in the room because I woke up so easily, and my job stress kept me up. She joked that I had to find some way to sleep while I'm writing since I just naturally don't notice anything around me when I'm in the midst of writing.

That day, I was writing about the culture of Paul's day and comparing it to our modern culture and the effects on our theology and sermon messages. I love culture and have written two books about it, so I was feeling right in the depths of my soul or my calling—and then the dream I had the night before started to make sense!

I dreamed that there was a very deep hole that I thought that my kids had dug but then I looked closely, and it was waaay deeper than they could have dug and must have been dug by one of those big construction bulldozers with the big shovel (called excavators). There was water running on top, but I looked way down at the bottom and it looked like there was also water running at the bottom—an underground stream. It wasn't deep or fast, just a small, shallow, quiet stream. It seemed to be in a pair, one on both sides at the top and bottom of the hole.

This dream reminded me of the phrase that still waters run deep, so I looked it up on the internet, and it means a quiet person that is passionate on the inside—that is totally me!! Water, ice, and snow are frequently symbols for emotion in my dreams. The streams were small and quiet and in a pair at the top and the bottom of the hole, symbolizing a peaceful emotional balance on the surface and deep inside. Water is also a symbol for the Holy Spirit. These streams symbolize His thirst-quenching, satisfying Spirit flowing both outside and deep inside me.

In my dream, I thought my kids had dug the hole. I frequently tell my wife how much joy my kids give me. However, in my dream the hole wasn't something that my children had dug. In my dream there was an excavator, so I looked up some synonyms for excavate and found: mine, quarry, exhume, and unearth. And then it hit me, the shovel (excavator) in my dream was symbolic of the work I do in unearthing the truth and digging for depths of insight—which is something I am passionate about and really excites me. One person commented, "This level of discernment could never have been achieved through the use of a dream dictionary, as it touches your spirit in a very personal way."

I once did a special assignment for two months as a reporter for an Army base newspaper. It was an interesting job and I had several writing assignments, but the only time I had that 'in the zone' feeling was when I was writing articles about toxic leadership in the Army. These articles were based on my personal experiences and spoke truth into a dysfunctional Army culture.

In my dream, I was surprised how deep the hole was, and to a lesser extent, that waters were running at the bottom. One online dictionary states, "If you dream of being happily surprised, you are beginning to acknowledge your unconscious feelings." This dream was about the passion I rediscovered through writing with depth of insight and about truth.

Spirit and Truth

My great-grandfather was the Methodist minister in northern Texas, and it was extremely cold in the winter and many people had no fuel for heat. He supposedly organized a group of vigilantes, and they stopped the train and stole coal from the train so people could have some heat in their homes. I have to admit that I resonate with him, and I wonder where to draw the line on standing up for what is right.

Those who are filled with the Holy Spirit bear the fruit of the Spirit: "But the fruit of the Spirit is love, joy, peace, patience, kindness, goodness, faithfulness, gentleness, self-control; against such things there is no law" (Galatians 5:22-23).

John Wesley's sermon on Scriptural Christianity seems to address the question of Spirit and truth. "Have we a bitter zeal, inciting us to strive sharply and passionately with them that are out of the way? Or is our zeal the flame of love, so as to direct all our words with sweetness, lowliness, and meekness of wisdom?"

The bitter zeal Wesley refers to is James 3:14:
"But if ye have bitter envying and strife in your hearts, glory not, and lie not against the truth."

"If ye have bitter zeal — True Christian zeal is only the flame of love. Even in your hearts - Though it went no farther."

"Do not lie against the truth — As if such zeal could consist with heavenly wisdom."

Does our tone demonstrate our lack of the fruit of the Holy Spirit: kind, patient, long suffering? Love is not puffed up, it is humble, lowly and meek. Truth can come from people not demonstrating the gifts or the fruit of the Holy Spirit, but that doesn't mean God approves. The Holy Spirit is the Spirit of Truth.

In speaking the truth we risk fortune, liberty, and life, and many will reject us. "And do ye not count your fortune, liberty, life, dear unto your selves, so ye may be instrumental in the restoring of it? But suppose ye have this desire, who hath any power proportioned to the effect ? Perhaps some of you have made a few faint attempts, but with how small success! Shall Christianity then be restored by young, unknown, inconsiderable men? I know not whether ye yourselves could suffer it. Would not some of you cry out, 'Young man, in so doing thou reproachest us'?"

On the other hand, there are so few who really stand for the truth in our culture that we are slipping beyond man's reproach into the judgment of God. "But there is no danger of your being put to the proof; so hath iniquity overspread us like a flood. Whom then shall God send?—the famine, the pestilence (the last messengers of God to a guilty land), or the sword, 'the armies of the' Romish 'aliens,' to reform us into our first love? Nay, 'rather let us fall into Thy hand, O Lord, and let us not fall into the hand of man.'"

"Whosoever heareth the sound of the trumpet, and taketh not warning; if the sword come, and take him away, his blood shall be upon his own head." (Ezek. 33:4).

2

Leadings

We can't talk about dreams or visions without talking about some of the other ways that the Lord speaks to us, guides us, and leads us.

Here is an example of one of Billy Graham's leadings from the Holy Spirit:

"Sometime toward the end of the second week in November (in 1963), I unaccountably felt such a burden about the presidential visit to Dallas that I decided to phone our mutual friend, Senator Smathers, to tell him I really wanted to talk to the President. His secretary told me Senator Smathers was on the Senate floor and would call me back. Instead, he sent me a telegram that the President would get in touch with me directly. He thought I wanted to talk about the President's invitation to another golf game in Florida that weekend; the game was off, he said, and would have to be rescheduled.

But all I wanted to tell him and the President was one thing: "Don't go to Texas!"

I had an inner foreboding that something terrible was going to happen...But was such a strange feeling enough to justify the President's attention?" (from the book *Just As I Am* by Billy Graham)

> *All I wanted to tell him and the President was one thing: "Don't go to Texas!".*

One person commented, "There was much going on spiritually leading up to my mother's death. Leadings, visions, and even songs. I was led to call her at 10:00 P.M. I knew it was a bit late to be calling, but I had just found some genealogy information online that I wanted to share with Mom. She was still awake, and we talked and laughed. Something in me prompted me to hold on to that laughter, remembering it over and over. That was the last time that we spoke."

Premonitions

I definitely think the Holy Spirit gives us leadings about people we are close to. This same person commented, "I am sure of it. I have even had leadings about those whom are acquaintances, but not close to me. A few years ago I felt that the man we purchased our sheep guardian llama from had been taken by EMS to the hospital. Sometime afterwards I ran into his wife at the grocery store, and she told me that had happened."

"One morning I felt that another farmer we know had a traffic accident in the fog when a driver hit him in his truck. I saw a red truck, but it was his black truck in the accident that same morning in the fog. Even though the color did not match, the vision had taken place. Perhaps the red truck denoted danger?"

"This summer I kept having a vague feeling about danger to a left arm. I hoped it wasn't mine! Then I thought that perhaps it was someone else's left arm in danger and felt worried. Shortly thereafter, my husband's nephew who lives just up the road from us, had an accident in his car where he was thrown from the vehicle and suffered a severe break in his left arm. He had surgery to fix it and thought it was healing nicely, but required another surgery recently."

"One day I was pulling weeds around our chicken coop. Our son was mowing the front yard on the riding lawn mower. We have several old, large trees in our yard. He was mowing under the big maple tree at the time. I was suddenly prompted to stop him and ask him to go now to the barn at his grandmother's and get a tool that we needed to use. He got off the mower and headed up the road in his truck. No sooner had he passed the maple tree than a huge branch fell to the ground where he had been mowing. Coincidence? I don't think so. Perhaps we need to be bolder in our conviction of our dreams and visions so that we could possibly spare someone heartache or danger."

I find that songs and sermons are one of the places that the Lord uses repetition to make a point. Maybe I will hear something in a sermon and then someone will say something, and later a song comes to mind that seems to repeat that particular point—something God is trying to say to me.

Carefully Listen and Obey

In the Bible the Lord told people when and where to attack the enemy or to lay and wait:

"When David inquired of the LORD, He said, "You shall not go directly up; circle around behind them and come at them in front of the balsam trees. "It shall be, when you hear the sound of marching in the tops of the balsam trees, then you shall act promptly, for then the LORD will have gone out before you to strike the army of the Philistines." Then David did so, just as the LORD had commanded him, and struck down the Philistines from Geba as far as Gezer" (2 Samuel 5:23-25).

David followed the Lord's detailed instructions. Saul, on the other hand, didn't wait on God's timing or listen to God's specific instructions and suffered the consequences (see 1 Samuel 13). There were many times during spiritual battles at work that I would listen to the leading of the Lord in my spirit giving me a specific time or day to speak the truth or take some action.

"Your own ears will hear him. Right behind you a voice will say, "This is the way you should go," whether to the right or to the left" (Isaiah 30:21).

When I was living in Alaska, I was applying for developmental assignments within the Army. I decided to apply for assignments in Hawaii, Italy and Korea because I love to travel and wanted to get away from my workplace, and

Alaska. I was applying for Public Affairs positions, and there was also one on the base where I worked, but I didn't want to stay there for an assignment. However, I kept feeling like the Lord was telling me to apply for that local assignment. I had several days to apply, so I dragged my feet but finally gave in and applied for the local assignment in addition to the international ones, although I ranked it as my last choice on the application.

Six months later I got a word during prayer three times to "go forth". I checked my email, and there were the results for the developmental assignment with my name listed as an awardee to a local assignment—because of Army budget cuts all assignments were local that year. He told me to apply for the local assignment even though I didn't want to and struggled against it but was obedient—and sure enough something I couldn't foresee happened. Many times following His leadings are a step of faith and intended to increase my ability to hear the Lord and trust Him even when it's contrary to my desire or even common sense.

It's hard to describe, but a lot of times the Lord will guide me on "whether to go to the right or to the left" by giving me a sort of slight nausea or a little dizzy feeling when I'm headed in the wrong direction. My thinking also sometimes becomes fuzzy or forgetful, which is an indicator that I am headed in the wrong direction. And sometimes, when I'm trying to check in my spirit for an answer or direction, and there is an absence of these kinds of feelings, I know I'm on the right track—I don't sense a hinderance in my spirit. People call leadings different things like checks in your spirit, conviction, and inner witness. Basically it's a feeling in your spirit telling whether something is right or wrong.

Simple leadings

In my experience the Lord can lead me in simple decisions every day, and I'm not sure what the outcome is, but I trust He is leading me and I don't have to test whether it's from Him or not. For example, I was choosing my clothes for the day and felt led to wear something warm. On my lunch break I went to the gym and found out it was closed, so I had to go ice-skating instead, which requires warmer clothes.

Another example of a simple leading was a big project I was working on that was due the next day at work. I needed some help, so at 1:42 p.m. I emailed someone that worked at headquarters, which was in another state and in a time zone that was three hours later. I only had a few hours left and I didn't think I had time to wait for their response, but the Lord told me to wait and not go off and do something else. It wasn't easy, because I had doubts about finishing the project on time, but sure enough they responded at 3:18 p.m. I got the information I needed, the project finished a lot quicker than I thought, and I was done with time to spare. The Lord knew exactly how much time I needed to get done and used this opportunity to grow and stretch my faith in his leading.

On my second day of work in the Public Affairs office, they had been trying to micromanage me in making a newspaper interview appointment. I still didn't have a telephone line yet, but I felt the Lord telling me to wait until 9:00 a.m. to make the call for the appointment. A few minutes before 9:00 a.m., I heard the editor talking on the phone saying that the interviewee was out sick yesterday and today. I was seriously amazed at the Lord's leading in battle. I didn't have to go into the big deal of taking my phone into the other office, and plug it in where another guy was, and try to make this appointment. But even more miraculous was that at exactly

9:00 a.m.—to the minute—the editor walked in and told me he was out sick so I didn't have to bother making the phone call.

I have had many of these leadings in my spirit where the Lord is telling me what day and time to take a certain course of action. Many times I have simple leadings in my spirit that tell me whether to act or wait, and when and how. Others have commented that they don't have these simple kind of leadings. I've never had, or at least recognized, a dream about national events—of course, I don't follow national events very closely either. One person who had dreams about national events said she also didn't follow national events but felt it was God saying, "Pay attention!" The Lord works with each of us in unique ways.

Revealing the Unseen

A leading can be something the Lord brings to mind. When I was a teen I spent a day away from home and kept thinking about my older brother for some reason. I found out later that day he got a concussion at school in gym class (and recovered fine).

One person commented, "Years ago I woke up with the name in my spirit of a girl who graduated from our school a year before I did. I had not thought of her for years. I then found out that she had passed away two weeks prior to my receiving her name. I think that my Grandmother wanted me to know that since she was a distant cousin on her side of the family."

"A few months ago, a man's last name popped into my mind one afternoon. I had no reason to think of this name. As I logged into my email I saw a message from someone who sends local news from a small town where I used to live. I clicked on the message and read that Mr. McKinney, a resident of that town, had passed away. This was the name that had come to my mind right before I turned on the computer."

Lessons from leadings

Leadings can also happen after the fact to show us ourselves. It wasn't until after Peter had betrayed Jesus three times that the Lord brought to his mind the words He prophesied about Peter. "And Peter remembered the saying of Jesus, 'Before the rooster crows, you will deny me three times'" (Matthew 26:17). The same thing can happen with dreams. We will remember a dream after something has already taken place and that dream may be showing us something about ourselves.

"The secrets of his heart are disclosed, and so, falling on his face, he will worship God and declare that God is really among you" (1 Cor. 14:25).

One day I took my usual walk on break and went down by the river. I raised my hands and started praying and heard a cracking of sticks behind me. I turned around and about thirty feet away was something in the trees. I thought it was a moose and got scared since they sometimes charge, but it wasn't tall like a moose, it was lower to the ground. Was it a person or a dog? No, it was too big for that, and the way it moved was different, and it was dark colored. I thought it was a bear! In a panic I asked God what to do, but I didn't feel any leading.

I could back up the path I had just come down, but that led in the direction of the animal, or I could proceed on the path that shortly ended at the frozen river. It didn't make sense to get any closer, so I reacted and went down the river path and scurried along on the frozen river (even though it had been a warm 30's for several days, and the ice was probably getting thin). Down-a-ways I scrambled back up the bank and went up the road back to where I came from.

I believe He was telling me not to give into my fear and wait for His leading—even in the absence of His leading. At the time, there were many situations at work that I needed to wait and trust in the Lord's leading—and He used this situation to make that clear. I came back a day or so later and saw some broken branches and moose droppings on the ground. Moose aren't as dangerous as bears, and I realized that I could have waited on the Lord's leading.

Burdens

> But if I say, "I will not mention his word or speak anymore in his name," his word is in my heart like a fire, a fire shut up in my bones. I am weary of holding it in; indeed, I cannot (Jeremiah 20:9).

The Lord will guide us through burdens. Sometimes I will get a burden from the Lord about something that needs to be addressed in my family, workplace, or church. I find that the Lord will many times confirm His leading and that burden through my daily reading of scripture. There will be certain verses that speak to my situation and offer comfort and encouragement as I speak a word of correction to someone.

Many people will ignore a burden in order to avoid conflict, but that is being unfaithful to the Lord's leading. Many times when we address problems (that the Lord has called us to address), we will face the same retaliation Jesus and the prophets faced in the Bible.

I had a burden to email the pastor of our church when we lived in Alaska. I didn't want to do this because I knew what had to be said wouldn't be received well. I delayed for about a week, until, much like Jonah, I knew I couldn't avoid it—the burden just got more grievous, so I finally sent the email.

Several days after I sent the email, I found out there had been a members' meeting to vote on the expansion of the church. If I had been obedient and sent that email when the Lord was telling me to, it would have arrived before they made the decision to expand the church. The email wasn't about the expansion of the church (I didn't even know they were voting on that), but instead the need for more authentic Christianity within the church—something a larger building wouldn't solve.

Words to Speak

I have also found that God is true to His Word and will give us the words to speak when the time comes, so we don't have to worry or obsess about possible scenarios and how we will reply.

"And when they bring you before the synagogues and the rulers and the authorities, do not be anxious about how you should defend yourself or what you should say, for the Holy Spirit will teach you in that very hour what you ought to say" (Luke 12:11-12).

The Lord led me to have a meeting with one of our church leadership to talk about cessationism. I hadn't realized it, but the Lord had prepared me the previous couple weeks through the things He showed me in my research on the internet. In particular was an article about John Piper's bad experience with false prophecy. The person I talked to brought up that exact story, so I was prepared to respond that it appears many cessationists (and continuationists) have had similar bad experiences—but they are partly responsible because they fail to train up prophets in the way they should go.

A couple months after I met with the pastor, I met with the elder board over the false doctrine of cessationism in the church. The Lord came through and prepared me with answers to all their questions, accusations and attacks. He prepared me over the previous few months and right before the meeting with various topics they raised. I didn't go out of my way to prepare a defense or to study up on all the different viewpoints trying to anticipate their arguments. The Lord was faithful to His promise and through the course of daily events taught me everything I needed to say.

The elders opened the meeting with the question of disunity, which seems to be the standard reaction when you try to correct or confront something in the American church. Just the week or two before, I had read an article about the disunity verse (Romans 16:17). I told them that verse on disunity in the Bible talks about false doctrine. It's false doctrine, the very thing I was addressing, which causes disunity.

On Saturday, the day before the meeting with the elders, my son was listening to Chris Tomlin's 'Our God' song on his iPad, so I listened to it too. It was one of the first songs I learned at this church, so I associated it with this church. I was singing it throughout the day:

"Into the darkness you shine, out of the ashes we rise, there's no one like you, none like You!

Our God is greater, our God is stronger, God you are higher than any other.

Our God is Healer, Awesome in Power, Our God! Our God!

And if our God is for us, then who could ever stop us?

And if our God is with us, then what could stand against?

And if our God is for us, then who could ever stop us?

And if our God is with us, then what could stand against?

What could stand against?"

I listened to my daily scripture reading plan the next morning. It was on Romans chapter eight, and of course I was surprised to hear the very verse I had been singing the day before. I went to church that morning, and guess what was printed on the front of the church bulletin! "What then shall we say to these things? If God is for us, who can be against us?" (Romans 8:31).

My meeting with the elders was right after the service. He was true to His promise, He prepared me for that meeting and He stood for me in that meeting, and their attacks did not prevail. If we are careful to listen to His voice in all the ways He speaks to us and obedient to follow His leadings, who or what can stand against us?

Prophetic Hints

"When the Spirit of truth comes, he will guide you into all the truth, for he will not speak on his own authority, but whatever he hears he will speak, and he will declare to you the things that are to come" (John 16:13).

It isn't just through dreams and visions that the Lord declares to people things that are to come. The Lord will bring about prophetic hints of what is going to happen in our everyday life. In Isaiah 8:1-4, God tells Isaiah to write a name on a tablet, and then have a son and give him that name. The meaning of the child's name was a prophetic hint foretelling the taking and dividing of spoils (the invasion of Israel by Assyria) that would take place in the child's life.

One person reported a prophetic hint they experienced, "Do you remember when Haiti experienced those horrible earthquakes? The morning of the earthquake, I had just awakened and heard a loud noise and felt a slight vibration. We don't typically have earthquakes here in Ohio, so I thought it might have been the stone quarry 5 miles away blasting, but it was Sunday morning. My husband and son did not hear it, and numerous searches online didn't show any seismic activity for our area. Then I heard the news about the earthquakes in Haiti. I believe that God was telling me what had happened in a way that He had not communicated with me before...with actual physical manifestations."

I have a place where I ride my bike to and hike into the forest a little ways and pray at a spot that overlooks a ravine. There have been several times the Lord has given me a prophetic hint as to what was going to happen that week—especially during difficult times. For example, one Tuesday afternoon I was praying there, and I heard all kinds of guns shooting and an explosion that might have been a grenade. I was surprised because in the years that I have been coming to this spot it was the first time I heard this. I found out later it was some military exercises at the neighboring base, but it sounded like it was just on the other side of the mountain where I was standing. This was unusual, and I wondered if it was a prophetic hint for the upcoming week.

A couple days later the pastor of our new church called me and asked if I wanted to drive up together to the men's retreat the next day, and I said yes. The sermon at the retreat Friday night was on spiritual warfare. I took notes but didn't really feel like it was speaking to my situation.

I had met with our new pastor two times in the past two weeks and discussed what had happened at our last church with me confronting their cessationism. The conversation continued between us during our ride share back and forth Friday night. The pastor said some things I didn't agree with, and on Saturday morning the conversation escalated to the point of an argument that lasted about an hour and a half and ended with him deciding to drive me back home. He completely disagreed with what I did at our old church and made some other comments about me. It turned out He was old friends with the pastor I confronted. I told him he was like King Jehoshaphat: a godly man doing godly things, but had ungodly alliance (with that pastor).

After getting home I remembered from that spiritual warfare sermon that we are to take time to relax and go to the beach, so that's exactly what I did with my family. As I was feeling relaxed sitting on the beach, I suddenly recalled the prophetic hint He had shown me on Tuesday at my forest prayer spot. Through this prophetic hint and the sermon on Friday, God had foreshadowed and prepared me for the spiritual warfare that would happen with this pastor.

At that point I knew He was in control, and any doubts I had about what had happened left me. I had been true to the conviction in my heart, and according what the sermon had taught, I took responsibility for resisting the deception and cunning of the devil and standing firm in the truth. Pastors are not above reproach, even godly men can have areas of their life that they are sinning. "God wants you to speak up for what you know is right. Speak up even when it is hard." (Adventure Bible).

> *I had been true to the conviction in my heart and standing firm in the truth.*

3

Symbols

W hy does God use symbols in dreams instead of giving us a literal message? It's probably the same reason He used parables. He reveals himself to those who have an open heart to Him. The secrets of the Kingdom of God are only going to be given to those who have an open heart (see Luke 8:10). And to those that have a closed heart He will take away even what they think they understand.

> "So pay attention to how you hear. To those who listen to my teaching, more understanding will be given. But for those who are not listening, even what they think they understand will be taken away from them" (Luke 8:18).

"The word heart (by coincidence) starts with the word hear. The good heart hears God's word and understands it" (www.simplybible.com). Not only is it a matter of a good heart, it's a matter of God's timing:

"Listen to me and remember what I say. The Son of Man is going to be betrayed into the hands of his enemies." But they didn't know what he meant. Its significance was hidden from them, so they couldn't understand it, and they were afraid to ask him about it" (Luke 9:44-45).

Listen and remember your dream, and maybe later, according to God's timing, He will reveal the true meaning to you. This happened to me with an anger warning dream. Right as I was about to speak out in anger, I suddenly remembered my dream, and all the symbols in the dream fit my exact circumstances at the time.

One person commented, "I have come to the conclusion that at least one of the reasons the dreams occur this way is to give us layers of meaning, not just a cut and dry statement that something is going to occur. Since I used to draw and paint when time permitted, I love imagery, color, and the feelings that can be derived from them."

Did you notice the cover of this book? Did you recognize it as a scene from the Bible? Did you think it was Moses and Pharaoh? It's a painting by Adrien Guignet depicting Joseph explaining Pharaoh's dream. Someone who isn't a Christian probably wouldn't have known the story of Joseph or understood what this painting depicts. Some believe God will reveal to you the meaning of your dreams and we don't have to work at understanding them, but even the disciples had to work at understanding the parables Jesus told.

He did not speak to them without a parable, but privately to his own disciples he explained everything (Mark 4:34).

Personal Meaning

By 2009, I had written in total about sixteen blog entries on dreams. I didn't get a lot of traffic to my website, but people searching for 'Christian dream interpretation' was one of the top three searches people come to my blog for. I also received several comments from people asking what their dream meant. However, I usually ended up explaining that people have to learn to interpret their own dreams because only they really understand what all the symbols mean to them. If they pray to God for Him to show them the meaning of their dream, in my experience, He is faithful in doing so.

For example, you would think I would know my wife well enough to interpret her dreams. My wife had a dream of her sister chasing her. I had no idea what her sister represented to her. She felt her sister represented a professional working woman to her. At the time, my wife was applying for part-time work, and her dream showed how she was running from that. Her sister is now married and stays at home, so she would symbolize something else if my wife had a dream about her today.

"I want to let you know that dreams which involve people we know are almost never about them, but about characteristics within us that they symbolize for us. Many people who are prophetically gifted or very empathetic quickly jump to the conclusion that they have received some important insight into another person. Perhaps so, but don't assume it from the start" (Herman Riffel, Dream Journaling article).

One person looked up the symbols from Pharaoh's dream (Genesis 41), and the interpretation didn't match any dream dictionaries. Symbols are different for different people, at different times in their lives, and different cultures, and different periods of history. Personal meaning for a symbol is something you won't find in a dream dictionary—instead it's something the Lord shows you, just like the disciples turned to Jesus for the interpretation of His parables.

Windows dream

The following person recognized a symbol in her dream that had been repeated in other dreams and discovered what that symbol meant to her personally:

"Since the dream I was given the morning of my mother's heart attack, which rendered her unconscious for the remaining 3 weeks of her life, was also through our 4 living room windows, I have pondered why the Lord was showing me these things through windows. I searched backwards in time through my life and recalled something that happened when I was 9 years old.

> *I have pondered why the Lord was showing me these things through windows.*

"My brother, who was 8 years old at the time, suffered compound skull fractures in a farm accident at another child's home during Christmas vacation. He was in intensive care for some time, but eventually recovered. I remember one morning during this time, waiting for the school bus with my sister, aged 10, on our enclosed back porch. There was a window from this porch to the living room. As the bus pulled into the driveway of our farm, I looked through the window and saw my young mother sitting in a chair, sobbing uncontrollably.

"I ignored the school bus waiting for me and went back into the living room and stood by my mother. She told me to go ahead and get on the bus, and that she would be all right. Somehow, I feel that this is connected to our Heavenly Father showing me these two visions through windows. I had blocked out what was going on in my everyday life to go stand at my mother's side."

Hawaii transition dream

My son had this dream in 2012 when we were living in Alaska and demonstrates how symbols are personal to each individual:

My son dreamed he was in a nice hotel. He said it felt like it was near a beach, and maybe there was a little sand and there was a little snow. He was looking out the window, and there were several planes flying by: three F-22 raptors, one super carrier, one B-2 bomber, and then five passenger planes—ten planes in all. He wanted to run down and look at them from outside the hotel but didn't want to miss them, so he watched them from the window.

I explained to him a hotel meant a life transition, but we couldn't figure out what the planes meant. We prayed about it that evening when he mentioned the dream again, and God was faithful in showing him the meaning.

After we prayed we we're talking, he looked up at his bookshelf and saw his boat from his Cub Scout boat race. That reminded him of the Cub Scout pinewood derby and he realized the planes in his dream were symbols for derby cars. He was just as excited about the upcoming pinewood derby as he was about seeing those planes in his dream. It was going to be his first derby in Alaska.

I told my wife about it, and she asked what the hotel meant. I said transitions and mentioned that he was excited that it was his first race in Alaska, and then I realized it was a transition from his old Cub Scout pack in Hawaii to his new Webelos pack in Alaska, and this was their first major event.

It was kind of unusual for my son to be so interested in what his dream meant and to bring it up again, and it seemed to have a significant impression on him, so I thought this must be something God was saying. Maybe a message to me on how important this derby event was to him? He even came in second place for the Webelos den but was still disappointed. He also ended up with an extra pinewood car block and already wanted to start working on shaping it for the next year.

The beach with a little sand and little snow outside the hotel in his dream was about his transition from Hawaii to Alaska. This dream occurred about fourteen months after we had moved to Alaska. He didn't want to leave Hawaii, but became very attached to Alaska, and after we moved back to Hawaii he still very much wanted to live in Alaska.

Difficulty with Symbols

People in our American culture have a problem with dreams because we aren't taught the language of dreams. "Schools taught us to learn the language of reason and neglect the language of symbols. Jesus said we must become like children to understand Him. Learning to understand the key role that symbolic language has in dream interpretation is the first step in understanding how the dream speaks" (Herman Riffel, Dream Dictionaries article).

I wrote a book that examined the cultures of the world and found that not all cultures are reasoning and analytical. Some other cultures in the world, such as Middle-Eastern culture, my be more fluent in this language of symbols and therefore more receptive to dreams. Maybe this is why we feel, as Americans, we have to rely on dream dictionaries.

One person commented, "Most people have a difficult time viewing things symbolically. They only see the literal meaning of anything. There are those whose ability to symbolize is more refined, such as artists, poets, writers, and others who possess much creativity. We have all heard the saying "a picture is worth a thousand words." The same is true concerning dreams from God. He can pack much more meaning in a single image or symbol than He could if He literally spoke words to us.

When I have had dreams with multiple images and colors, they are loaded with information and significance. All this takes place in mere seconds. To write a summary of these dreams in words would take much longer and be several pages or even chapters long with the more intricate dreams and interpretations with layers upon layers of various meanings. Why would God not understand our abilities to assimilate what He says to us, using the best method? After all, He created our brains, our hearts, and our spirits."

No dream dictionaries

Many people try to use dream dictionaries to find the meaning of symbols in their dreams. One conviction I had, as I was writing and researching for this book, was to try to listen to the Lord instead of using dream dictionaries. This book is the result of many years of dream journaling and research so it still contains a few references to dream dictionaries.

Herman Riffel, the author of *Dream Interpretation: A Biblical Understanding*, believes that dream dictionaries shouldn't be used at all: "There is much to learn about dreams, and in order to interpret the meaning of a dream there is a great temptation to turn to a dream dictionary to find the meaning of the symbols in the dream, or to seek someone who has devised a pattern to quickly get an interpretation of the dream. Though I, too, at first wanted that, I found that it is one of the serious traps in dream interpretation. It causes us to jump to false conclusions and focus on the meaning that we want the dream to have rather than what God may actually be revealing. By turning to dream dictionaries or patterns one is avoiding listening to God, in the heart or unconscious, to hear what God is saying, and instead depending on another person's ideas, and missing the point that God is making."

No one in the Bible ever used a dream dictionary. One person commented, "Many years ago my mother purchased dream dictionaries, and we used to look up the meanings of our dreams. Although she had no prophetic dreams of which I'm aware, she had a strong belief in the prophetic nature of dreams. I gave up on dream dictionaries long ago and find that the complexity of my dreams could not be explained in this way."

Herman Riffel, in a Dream Dictionaries article, said, "I do not find any pattern in the Scriptures of having classes to interpret dreams, though there were classes for prophets. I did have classes like that and tried to get people to listen to their hearts for the meaning of the dreams. However, I was disillusioned with that, for people at first were interested, but then very, very few would follow through in learning to listen privately to God for the meaning of their dreams."

I stopped using dream dictionaries when I started writing this book and after reading Riffel's comments on dream dictionaries. Now that I have stopped using a dream dictionary, the Lord has revealed the meaning of my dreams even more clearly.

Riffel's book was one of the first Christian dream interpretation books I read—when I was still into Jungian psychology. Riffel uses quite a bit of Jungian psychology in his book. However, I don't believe we should use Jungian psychology either. Also, many dream dictionaries have some of the original dream definitions created by Jung.

Learning how to hear God is the true key to understanding our dreams.

Learning how to hear God speaking into our lives is the true key to understanding our dreams. He can speak through scripture, dreams, circumstances, friends, fellow Christians, church-members, our spouse, etc.

"Without consultation, plans are frustrated, but with many counselors they succeed" (Proverbs 15:22).

4

Discernment

The Billy Graham Evangelistic Association website has several articles authored by the BGEA staff with "thoughtful responses to a wide assortment of questions". One of the questions they try to answer is about dreams. Here is that article:

Does God reveal things through dreams and visions?

The Bible indicates that God revealed His will to selected people through dreams or visions in scriptures such as Genesis 37:5-10; 1 Kings 3:5-15; Daniel, chapters 2 and 7; Matthew 1:20; 2:13,19; and Acts 10:9-16; 16:9.

God may communicate through dreams or visions even today, but we need to carefully check any such guidance we receive with scripture and godly counsel to be sure it is from the Lord. Anything which contradicts scripture is not from God. Our minds and even Satan are capable of producing great deception in such subjective areas.

2 Timothy 3:16-17 shows that God has revealed His will to us primarily through His Word. It says, 'All Scripture is

God-breathed and is useful for teaching, rebuking, correcting and training in righteousness, so that the man of God may be thoroughly equipped for every good work'.

Here are a few comments made on that BGEA article:

"The sole purpose of God speaking to us through visions/dreams is to fulfill His will and/or to warn us. It is a supernatural thing that does not occur with regularity. God does not make it confusing to figure out. If it is, then it is not from God."

"I can say dreams sometimes are ways in which God communicates to us, especially in directing us to follow His will."

"I too have been having many visions and dreams. I've been having them for years now. Each one of them I draw and date. I sometimes go back to them, and that's when the revelation is revealed to me. Some of my dreams are confusing, and I ask God to show me the meaning of them; and He has. Most were about myself or a situation that's about to occur. It's up to us to seek and ask God for revelations. Sometimes those dreams we have can be meant for us to reevaluate ourselves in certain areas of our lives; to make change and trust Him"

"As long as the dream lines up with the Word of God... (Deuteronomy:1-3) If a prophet or a dreamer of dreams arises among you and gives you a sign or a wonder, and the sign or wonder that he tells you comes to pass, and if he says, 'Let us go after other gods,' which you have not known, 'and let us serve them,' you shall not listen to the words of that prophet or that dreamer of dreams."

Scripture First

The Bible should always be our first source for God's guidance. In the Bible, Gideon prayed for God to show him signs as confirmation of what he was supposed to do. "Today the greatest means of God's guidance is His Word, the Bible. Unlike Gideon, we have God's complete, revealed Word. If you want to have more of God's guidance, don't ask for signs; study the Bible" (Life Application Study Bible).

Dreams are messages from God, but they are not the Word of God. The Bible is the ultimate authority, and messages from God will not contradict it. Read the whole Bible, and spend more time studying it than you do your dreams.

"Let the prophet who has a dream tell the dream, but let him who has my word speak my word faithfully. What has straw in common with wheat? declares the Lord. Is not my word like fire, declares the Lord, and like a hammer that breaks the rock in pieces?" (Jeremiah 23:28).

Dreams are messages from God, but they are not the Word of God.

Someone said to me, "I don't believe we need to concentrate our efforts in translating or interpreting our dreams, but instead study God's word so we can learn what to listen for and have the ability to hear the Spirit and thus God's plans for the direction of our life."

I agree, God's word is much more important than dreams, however, we need to focus our efforts on hearing Him through all the ways available to us. We can't ignore the special way God speaks to believers (and non-believers) through their dreams.

False Discernment

We know from the Bible that the Lord God gives all interpretation to dreams. I don't know if He speaks to us through all our dreams, or if all our dreams are a message from Him, but I do know that to those whose ears are open to Him, He does speak frequently and in many different ways. However, we must also be careful not to seek Him in the wrong ways.

> *We don't need intermediaries, the Holy Spirit is all we need.*

"And when they say to you, "Inquire of the mediums and the necromancers who chirp and mutter," should not a people inquire of their God? Should they inquire of the dead on behalf of the living?" (Isaiah 8:19).

Shamanism is divination and soothsaying—which is strictly forbidden and considered evil by God. Divination and soothsaying is attempting to ascertain answers and the future through communication with spirits (and spirits of the dead—like Saul tried to do with a medium). Obviously, this is wicked because they are not God's spirit but spirits of the enemy.

"So Saul died for his breach of faith. He broke faith with the LORD in that he did not keep the command of the LORD, and also consulted a medium, seeking guidance. He did not seek guidance from the LORD. Therefore the LORD put him to death and turned the kingdom over to David the son of Jesse" (1 Chronicles 10:13-14 ESV).

If we seek the Lord with all our heart He will speak to us, and one of those ways is through dreams. And to some, He even gives the gift to prophesy, to speak a word to others given to them by God, sometimes through dreams, and sometimes telling the future.

One person commented, "The only thing in the chapter I didn't quite connect with was the broad reference to Shamanism. I felt you were more referring to Wiccan/Witchcraft sort of practices. I guess I take Shamanism to mean Native religions that revered the earth and taught reverence for all life. What do you think?"

I responded to that according to Wikipedia, "Shamanism encompasses the premise that shamans are intermediaries or messengers between the human world and the spirit worlds." We don't need intermediaries, the Holy Spirit is all we need.

False Sources

Herman Riffel wrote, "Nowhere in the Bible are we warned to be careful of dreams." However, Riffel found that some dreams can be from false sources. "As I spoke about dreams to a group of pastors in Singapore, some of them pointed out that their fathers had experienced dreams that told them not to listen to the missionaries. I was puzzled at first, but as we pointed out what God had said about those who go to idols, we soon recognized that this had happened because these older men had come from a corrupted Buddhist tradition; their dreams were influenced by these false sources."

We know that the Lord speaks to people through dreams who aren't filled with the Holy Spirit, like Pilate's wife whose dream made her tell Pilate not to persecute Jesus, or the Midianite soldier whose dream foretold Gideon's victory over the Midianites.

It's interesting how God spoke to non-believing, idol worshiping, King Nebuchadnezzar through his dreams but refused to speak to a believer, King Saul, because of his disobedience.

"And when Saul inquired of the LORD, the LORD did not answer him, either by dreams, or by Urim, or by prophets" (1 Samuel 28:6 ESV).
"Saul said, "God has turned away from me and answers me no more, either by prophets or by dreams"" (1 Samuel 28:15 ESV).

We also know there are many non-believers who claim God spoke to them in a dream. Mohammed, the founder of Islam, had many visions and dreams and so did Joseph

Smith, the founder of the Mormon church, so it's evident
the enemy also uses the visions and dreams of non-believers.

"I have heard what the prophets have said who
prophesy lies in my name, saying, 'I have dreamed,
I have dreamed!' How long shall there be lies in the
heart of the prophets who prophesy lies, and who
prophesy the deceit of their own heart" (Jeremiah
23:25-26).

False Philosophy

Radio and TV evangelist, R.C. Sproul believes only
dreams that really stand out have significance or are messages
from God. Sproul had a reoccurring dream about twenty
times and finally, after many years of having the dream, went
to a psychologist to help him understand it.

I don't believe we should turn to psychology for answers.
I sense an inherent deception in psychological theories and
terminology. For example, when I look up a word in the
dream dictionary, I find the psychological definitions are just
as misleading as the occult ones. I studied some of the Jungian
psychological theories—such as the dark side, and masculine
and feminine—and tried to understand my dreams using
these theories. I found they promise deeper understanding
but are actually a veil to the truth. And that's exactly how the
enemy works, he makes you think you're getting something
(like deeper understanding) but really takes it away.

When I stopped using Jungian personality types God
gave me a deeper understanding of others, and when I
stopped using Jungian interpretation of dreams, God gave
me a deeper understanding of my dreams. In my experience,

psychoanalysis of a dream only creates more confusion and instead of giving clarity, it actually clouds over the meaning.

God wants us to turn to Him for the answer. For example, Daniel asked God for the answer, and "during the night the mystery was revealed to Daniel in a vision" (Daniel 2:19). God gives us His promise in Jeremiah 33:3: "Call to me and I will answer you, and will tell you great and hidden things that you have not known".

Discernment and Culture

I've tried to develop my discernment by not watching things on TV that are going to dull my sensitivity. We don't subscribe to cable, and we are very careful what we watch on Netflix and YouTube.

"Forty years ago—when movies were relatively innocuous—Christians debated whether they should attend them. Now when they are largely objectionable, we are no longer asking the question...Don't live like Americans" (Snodgrass, NIV Application Commentary on Ephesians).

All the violence in the media and movies alone is enough to dull the senses, let alone hear the Holy Spirit. James 1:19 tells us the anger of man does not produce righteousness. James 1:27 says don't be stained by this world and Romans 12:2 says don't conform to this world, instead renew our minds, so we will be able to discern the will of God, which includes the ability to hear the Holy Spirit, which in turn affects our ability to hear Him through our dreams.

I try to stick to the Bible when I have time to read, and I only listen to Christian music. On the other hand, I felt the Lord also showed me in a dream that I shouldn't go to extremes either. One morning I woke up smiling because I was having a fun water fight in my dream.

I dreamed I was in the house of a blond haired guy who has killed someone before, and they haven't been able to arrest him yet. I tried to leave by saying I have something for him or want to show him something and head for the door. I have to work my way around something in the way that looks like glass chemistry experiment equipment. He was going towards the door as I did, and I was wondering if he will try to attack.

Next, I was sitting in a movie theatre about to watch a movie. A couple guys across the aisle did something in the projectionist box, and the projectionist was announcing the movie will not start until they come in there, apparently to get in trouble. In the seat next to me is the killer, and I want to distance myself from him.

Next he is gone, maybe inside the projectionist area, maybe because he was called in too? He left a huge long water gun. I stand up and shoot it and then shoot someone, and someone in a costume gets up to have fun and be shot by me. Next others in costumes (I think some are like Star Wars costumes) are standing up and shooting/squirting others. I am trying to shoot many people and having a great time.

I woke up the next morning (after having this dream) and I didn't have peace, because the day before I had cancelled my book on personality type and culture. I cancelled it because I felt that personality type was a gateway to the whole body of Jungian psychology. I believe there is much to be wary of in psychological theories.

One person thought the guy in my dream sounds like a mad scientist (with the chemistry set), this might be the part of me that goes to extremes in getting rid of (killing) things that I don't need to. The projection booth was my printer that I emailed the day before to cancel my book. That is why the 'movie' isn't playing. After not having peace about it and after this dream, I went ahead and told my printer to not cancel my personality type book after all.

When the mad scientist was gone I was having a wonderful time shooting/squirting others in the theatre. I don't like squirt guns that are shaped like guns, and we don't watch Star Wars because of the occult-like magic of 'the force'. I think the Lord was telling me I will enjoy life a little more if I lock up my mad scientist who is trying to kill off anything bad in our lives. Then I will wake up smiling like I did after this water gun fight in my dream.

A year before, I had a similar dream related to work. It was a scary dream where I was trying to kill this German guy by shooting a gun several times in his mouth, and it was causing some damage but not killing him.

At the time, God had been showing me some things about fear (vs. faith), and this dream showed I was being fearful and trying to control something by putting an end to it, but couldn't.

It was about an issue at work—a problem that I thought I had gotten rid of but my coworkers kept bringing back up. This was exactly what I feared would happen. He showed me through this dream about my fear and that the problem wasn't going to go away. And sure enough, that day, there was an email to several people (including myself) bringing up the problem again.

The German guy part of my dream was God telling me it was about my workplace, because one of my coworkers was

German and also involved in the problem that kept coming back up. It's not that I didn't like this person, it was simply God showing me, with typical dream amplification, how things were going—another example of the Lord's humor.

Like a radar beam that keeps a plane on track, prayer and dreams from God keep us alert to a potential problem, evil in a person or a situation, and sin in ourselves. He uses this to keep us in line with His purposes and to keep us following the leading of the Holy Spirit.

5

Dreams in the Bible

"And the Lord said to them, "Now listen to what I say: "If there were prophets among you, I, the Lord, would reveal myself in visions. I would speak to them in dreams. But not with my servant Moses. Of all my house, he is the one I trust. I speak to him face to face, clearly, and not in riddles!" (Numbers 12:6-8).

God has chosen to speak to us in the riddles of our dreams instead of face to face like He did with Moses. It wasn't just prophets that God spoke to through dreams, God spoke to all kinds of people throughout the Bible. There are 113 occurrences in the Bible for the word 'dream' and 118 occurrences for the word 'vision' in the NLT translation. The following is a list and categories of all the dreams I could find in the Bible that occurred before and after Pentecost.

Before Pentecost Dreams

Prophecy about one's own life.

1. In Abram's dream God promised the land of Israel to his descendants, and before that they would be enslaved for 400 years (see Genesis 15).

2. Joseph (son of Jacob) had a dream as a youth that his brothers' bundles of grain bowed down to his, which meant he would reign over his brothers (see Genesis 37).

3. In Joseph's second dream the sun, moon, and eleven stars bowed before him—symbols of his mother and father and eleven brothers. Later, the twelve brothers become the twelve tribes of Israel (see Genesis 37).

4. In Jacob's ladder or stairway dream God told Jacob He would give this land (Canaan) to his descendants and He will one day bring him back to this land (see Genesis 28:12).

5. A Midianite soldier had a dream of a loaf bread tumbling into their camp. It meant that Gideon would have victory over them (see Judges 7:13).

6. Solomon in his dream asked for wisdom and God gave him that, in addition to riches and fame (see 1 Kings 3).

Prophecy about one's own life interpreted by another.

There are also prophetic dreams about one's own life interpreted through someone with God's gift of dream interpretation. "God gave Daniel the special ability to interpret the meanings of visions and dreams" (Daniel 1:17). Joseph and Daniel were given the gift of interpretation of dreams—both of their own and others (i.e. Pharaoh and Nebuchadnezzar). This was before the Holy Spirit was given to us all. Now we can all hear from God the interpretation of our dreams—we look to the Holy Spirit to speak to our own hearts for the meaning of our dreams.

1. Joseph (son of Jacob) interpreted his jailmates' dreams. The cupbearer and baker's dreams of three branches and baskets mean in three days the Pharaoh would promote one and behead the other (see Genesis 40).

2. Joseph (son of Jacob) interpreted Pharaoh's dream of seven heads of wheat and seven cows as seven years of feast and famine (see Genesis 41).

3. Daniel interpreted Nebuchadnezzar's second dream of a large tree cut down and seven periods of time as symbolic of Nebuchadnezzar going insane for seven years (see Daniel 4).

God warns us.

1. God warns King Abimelech in a dream that he has been deceived and must give Abram his wife back or face destruction of his nation (see Genesis 20).

2. Laban (Jacob's father-in-law) is warned by God in a dream to not harm Jacob (see Genesis 31).

3. God warned the wise men in a dream not to tell Herod where the baby Jesus was (see Matthew 2:12).

4. Pilate's wife had a nightmare that Jesus was innocent and told her husband to leave him alone (see Matthew 27:19).

God commands or guides us.

1. Twenty years later, Jacob had a follow-up to his earlier personal prophecy dream. He had a dream where God told him that He has blessed his flocks and to return to the land of Canaan (see Genesis 31).

2. God told Joseph (husband of Mary) to flee to Egypt from Herod in Bethlehem (see Matthew 2:13).

3. An angel told Joseph (husband of Mary) to go back to Israel (see Matthew 2:19).

God informs us.

1. God told Joseph (husband of Mary) that Mary was pregnant by the Holy Spirit with the son of God—who is to be named Jesus (see Matthew 1:20).

There is a God in heaven who reveals secrets.

Gift of prophecy.

These are dreams that go beyond the normal limited scope of our lives, for example, to prophesy about whole countries, the world, and apocalyptic events (apocalyptic means symbolically predictive of future events). Even non-believers are given supernaturally prophetic dreams. "But there is a God in heaven who reveals secrets, and He has shown King Nebuchadnezzar what will happen in the future" (Daniel 2:28).

1. Daniel interpreted King Nebuchadnezzar's dream of a gold, silver, bronze, and iron statue as symbolic of four kingdoms ruling the world before an everlasting kingdom (see Daniel 2).
2. Daniel dreamt of four animals that represent four kingdoms that come before the kingdom of Christ. God told Him that this dream is about events in the distant future (see Daniel 7).
3. In a dream Jeremiah is told of God restoring Israel after exile to Babylon (see Jeremiah 31:23-26).

Visions before Pentecost.

Ezekiel's apocalyptic prophecy was a vision instead of a dream. Zechariah had prophecies about the reconstruction of the temple. In Zechariah 4:1 he says an angel woke him as if he had been asleep. I don't know if this counts as a dream or not.

After Pentecost Dreams

In the New Testament (after Pentecost) Paul, Ananias, Cornelius, Peter, and others, had visions from God. Some of Paul's visions were at night time:

"And a vision appeared to Paul in the night: a man of Macedonia was standing there, urging him and saying, 'Come over to Macedonia and help us'" (Acts 16:9).

"And the Lord said to Paul one night in a vision, 'Do not be afraid, but go on speaking and do not be silent," (Acts 18:9).

Nebuchanezzar had a dream and called it a vision, so it is fair to say that 'visions at night' are probably dreams:

"I saw a dream that made me afraid. As I lay in bed the fancies and the visions of my head alarmed me" (Daniel 4:5).

"From Paul on through the Middle Ages the church was never without men who used the gifts of wisdom and interpretation to understand dreams. Paul was only the first of many who made a conscientious effort to understand his dreams and, to a great extent, to govern his life by them" (Morton Kelsey).

Visions after Pentecost

1. The Lord told Ananias in a vision to go and pray for Saul (Paul) to receive his sight (see Acts 9:10).

2. The Lord told the gentile believer Cornelius to send for Peter so that even gentiles were saved (see Acts 10:3).

3. Peter fell into a trance and had a vision of food that the Lord used to tell him that even gentiles were to be accepted as believers (see Acts 10:10).

4. It appears John's book of Revelation wasn't a dream and came to him while he was exiled on the island of Patmos (for preaching the word of the Lord and for his testimony about Jesus). He was awake worshiping God in the Spirit, and a loud voice spoke to him, and he saw a vision (see Revelations 1:10).

Are Dreams for Today?

After Pentecost the Holy Spirit was given to all believers. Some people claim that God no longer speaks through dreams now that we have the Holy Spirit. However, Peter quoted the prophet Joel during the Pentecost outpouring of the Holy Spirit, declaring that when the Spirit is poured out, believers will prophesy, have dreams, and see visions.

"But Peter, standing with the eleven, lifted up his voice and addressed them: "Men of Judea and all who dwell in Jerusalem, let this be known to you, and give ear to my words. For these people are not drunk, as you suppose, since it is only the third hour of the day. But this is what was uttered through the prophet Joel:

"'And in the last days it shall be, God declares,
that I will pour out my Spirit on all flesh,
and your sons and your daughters shall prophesy,
and your young men shall see visions,
and your old men shall dream dreams;
even on my male servants and female servants
in those days I will pour out my Spirit,
and they shall prophesy.
And I will show wonders in the heavens above
and signs on the earth below,
blood, and fire, and vapor of smoke;
the sun shall be turned to darkness
and the moon to blood,
before the day of the Lord comes, the great and magnificent day.
And it shall come to pass that everyone who calls upon the name of the Lord shall be saved.'"
(Acts 2:14-21 ESV)

Peter is saying they are not drunk but this is the outpouring of the Holy Spirit foretold by the prophet Joel. This outpouring of the Holy Spirit includes prophesying, visions, and dreams. There are some who claim this verse is only about the end times and that we will only have visions and dreams during the end times. However, this was a dual prophecy about both Pentecost and Jesus' second coming.

Arnold and Beyer in *Encountering the Old Testament* (2008), state that prophecy can come in pairs with the first half telling of one event and the second half telling of a future event. For example, "Notice how Isaiah brought together Jesus' first and second comings in two adjacent verses. Verse 9:6 describes Jesus' first coming, whereas verse 7 describes His second coming. Prophets sometimes wrote in this way as they spoke of God's plans for the distant future."

> *Prophecy can come in pairs of near and distant future events.*

The same goes for Joel's prophecy quoted by Peter. It is two-fold like Isaiah's prophecy. Here are the original verses in Joel:

"And it shall come to pass afterward,
        that I will pour out my Spirit on all flesh;
    your sons and your daughters shall prophesy,
        your old men shall dream dreams,
        and your young men shall see visions.
    Even on the male and female servants
        in those days I will pour out my Spirit.

"And I will show wonders in the heavens and on the earth, blood and fire and columns of smoke. The sun shall be turned to darkness, and the moon to blood, before the great and awesome day of the LORD comes. And it shall come to pass that everyone who calls on the name of the LORD shall be saved. For in Mount Zion and in Jerusalem there shall be those who escape, as the LORD has said, and among the survivors shall be those whom the LORD calls" (Joel 2:28-32 ESV).

In the first part (set off in a poetry style in the Bible) the prophet Joel foretold the Pentecost outpouring of the Holy Spirit (along with prophesy, vision and dreams). In the second part (written in paragraph form in the Bible) he foretold of Jesus' second coming. Peter is telling us that prophecy, dreams and visions are for today and that in the future Jesus will come again.

> *Prophecy, dreams, and visions are for today.*

Peter's words (see below) demonstrate how closely tied together dreams and visions are to prophecy. This scripture starts and ends with 'pour out my Spirit' and 'will prophesy'. Notice what is sandwiched in between—dreams and visions are encapsulated *within* the prophecy of sons and daughters, and of men and women!

"'In the last days, God says,
I will pour out my Spirit on all people.

Your sons and daughters will prophesy,
your young men will see visions,
your old men will dream dreams.
Even on my servants, both men and women,
I will pour out my Spirit in those days,
and they will prophesy."
Acts 1:17-18

Dreams are for today! After the outpouring of the Holy
Spirit there were people filled with the Holy Spirit prophesying
and seeing visions.

John Wesley and Dreams

John Wesley was the founder of the Methodist church.
In 1749, Wesley testified that the spiritual gifts were for today
and even included dreams and visions in the list of spiritual
gifts! "The account given by St. Paul is a little fuller than
this: 'There are diversities of gifts' (carismavtwn, the usual
scriptural term for the miraculous gifts of the Holy Ghost),
'but the same Spirit. For to one is given the word of wisdom;
to another the gifts of healing; to another the working of'
other 'miracles; to another prophecy; to another discernment
of spirits; to another divers kinds of tongues; to another the
interpretation of tongues: all these worketh that one and the
same Spirit, dividing to every man severally as He will.' (1
Cor. xii. 4-11.)

Hence we may observe that the chief charismata, 'spiritual
gifts,' conferred on the apostolical Church were (1) casting out
devils; (2) speaking with new tongues; (3) escaping dangers,
in which otherwise they must have perished; (4) healing the

sick; (5) prophecy, foretelling things to come; (6) visions; (7) divine dreams; and (8) discerning of spirits.

Some of these appear to have been chiefly designed for the conviction of Jews and heathens, as the casting out devils and speaking with new tongues; some chiefly for the benefit of their fellow Christians, as healing the sick, foretelling things to come, and the discernment of spirits; and all in order to enable those who either wrought or saw them to 'run with patience the race set before them,' through all the storms of persecution which the most inveterate prejudice, rage, and malice could raise against them." (John Wesley's letter to Dr. Middleton 1749).

To the Ends of the Earth

Perry Stone, author of *How to Interpret Dreams and Visions*, believes dreams come from the flesh, the Spirit of God, and unclean spirits. Rabbi Kirt Schneider, of Discovering the Jewish Jesus, said most dreams are not from God but from our psyche, and some are from the enemy. Perry's 'flesh' and Schneider's 'psyche' seem to be the same thing. Herman Riffel was the author of many books including *Dream Interpretation* and *Learning to Hear God's Voice*. Riffel taught the Biblical interpretation of dreams for several decades and believed that all our dreams are messages from God—even the ones caused by the spicy food we ate the night before. I frequently have dreams where I only remember part of them but out of that fragment there is sometimes a complete message from God. Yet, I have many dreams I never come to understand the meaning of.

Riffel found that many pastors (of many different denominations) are not open to the idea of dream interpretation because it takes a willingness to break out of the security of what they already have and know. Sometimes the business of being a church becomes more important than inner growth, and many pastors have not experienced having to come to terms with their inner self. Riffel traveled through 50 countries, lecturing and presenting seminars on dreams to church leaders, missionaries, university professors, psychologists, and medical doctors. Riffel pointed out that western cultures aren't receptive to the idea of dream interpretation, whereas the rest of the world is.

Western culture tends to reject dreams or pass them off as psychological phenomenon; Middle-eastern culture appears to be more accepting of dreams as guidance from God. Many Muslims are coming to Christ through their dreams. One Vietnamese pastor said they evangelize the Muslims in Indonesia by first asking them if they have had any dreams. One academic author who was a long-term missionary in Indonesia said, "I have found Asian Christians far more likely to take seriously a dream as providing spiritual direction from God."

Muslims and dreams

One Sunday, I decided not to take my Bible to a Sunday school class on Islam because we weren't using them, but I felt a leading to bring a pen and paper. I didn't need to take notes in the first class and I didn't foresee taking notes, so I ignored that leading. Later in class, they talked about how Muslims are being led to Christ through dreams and visions, and someone mentioned an author. I wanted to check out that author, but I didn't have anything to write down the name. At that point, I knew I should have listened to His leading to bring a pen! I had to keep saying the author's name to myself so I wouldn't forget.

Fortunately, God was merciful and I didn't forget. It was Joel Rosenberg, the author of *Inside the Revival*. He has several testimonies of Muslims in Iran, West Bank, Saudi Arabia, and other Middle-Eastern countries coming to Christ through dreams and visions. Here are a few of those testimonies:

"I'm told that what is bringing these Iranians to Christ are dreams and visions of Jesus himself. Several years ago, an Iranian pastor I know met a twenty-two-year-old Iranian Shia woman who had become a Christian after seeing a vision of Jesus Christ. She just showed up in his church one day, hungry to study the Bible for herself."

"Just since 2007, nearly one thousand Muslims have come to Christ in the West Bank alone, most of them converted through dreams and visions of Jesus."

> *Jesus appeared to Marzuqah in a dream. 'Your prayers have been answered,' He told her.*

"A Saudi woman—let's call her Marzuqah (which means "blessed by God")—secretly converted to Christianity. But she had a brother who was dying of a terrible disease, and Marzuqah was deeply grieved. She prayed fervently for God to heal and to save her brother. One day, Jesus appeared to Marzuqah in a dream. 'Your prayers have been answered,' He told her. 'Go tell your brother about Me.' She did. To her astonishment, her brother prayed with her to receive Christ."

"Whole towns and villages along the Afghan-Pakistani border are seeing dreams and visions of Jesus and are converting to Christianity."

More than Dreams

There is an excellent DVD on Jesus' appearing to Muslims in dreams called More Than Dreams (2007) (www. morethandreams.tv). There are five remarkable testimonies of Muslims turning to Jesus. Each story is told in their native language. Here an excerpt of one testimony:

"Mohammed (Nigeria) - This Fulani herdsman in Nigeria found the deep love and lordship of Jesus Christ through a series of remarkable dreams. Jesus' appearance in those dreams altered the course of his life. Though his father tried to kill him in the wake of his conversion, he survived the various attempts on his life and eventually led his father to faith in Christ."

This Nigerian, after being a herdsman, went to school to study Islam and became the village expert and wanted to do even further studies of Islam until Jesus appeared to him in several dreams where Jesus saved him from his attackers.

The More Than Dreams DVD contains powerful and moving stories portraying the testimonies of Muslims in Egypt, Nigeria, Indonesia, Iran, and Turkey who have come to Jesus through both dreams and visions. On YouTube, there are also other videos with testimonies of Muslims coming to Christ through their dreams. We have friends, who were missionaries in Iraq for a couple years, who also saw Muslims coming to Christ through their dreams.

Jews and Dreams

Many Jews are now believing in Jesus, and the Jewish culture is more receptive to dreams. There is a program called the Jewish Jesus that has three episodes on Prophecy, Dreams, and Visions. In the program, Rabbi Kirt Schneider said God uses prophecy, dreams and visions to communicate to all people. He said most dreams are not from God but from our psyche. He said some dreams are from the enemy, ones that cause fear, betrayal, and division versus ones from God that give revelation and prepare us for victory. We have to pray and ask if a dream is from Him, to confirm it, to bring a witness one way or the other, and help us understand it (or we eventually forget about it).

He said every truth is taught in symbolic language/ parables, and visions are very simple, subtle word pictures that flash in our minds but share a thousand words. He said that in the Bible dreams are one of the most predominate ways God speaks to us. God uses dreams to communicate more often than any other way in the Bible. Through dreams God tells us that I AM with you and I AM going to see you through this thing.

6

Prognostic Dreams

Herman Riffel, in his book *Dream Interpretation: A Biblical Understanding*, explains that a "dream is pointing up our problem, or solution, or perhaps direction, or challenge or correction." Riffel says dreams can be warnings or promises. If we heed the warning we won't face the consequences, and if we keep from evil ways we will reap the rewards of the promises.

> For God speaks in one way,
> and in two, though man does not perceive it.
> In a dream, in a vision of the night,
> when deep sleep falls on men,
> while they slumber on their beds,
> then he opens the ears of men
> and terrifies them with warnings,
> that he may turn man aside from his deed
> and conceal pride from a man;
> he keeps back his soul from the pit,
> his life from perishing by the sword.
> Job 33:14-18

One pastor explained that God can call us to do something, and if we ignore Him there are two things that can happen. He passes us over and gives the opportunity to someone else (and we are given another assignment), or He takes from us (sometimes painfully depending on how tight our grip is) the very thing that is keeping us from obeying His will.

The example he gave was of Elijah when he ran away from Jezebel. He was sitting on a mountain complaining to God, and then God told him to go and appoint his successor Elisha. I have found that dreams are a very good place to hear God's warnings of the consequences of not obeying His will.

One atheist I know claims that he never has dreams; since dreams are the voice of God, it's not surprising that God isn't talking to him—because he isn't listening. If we ignore what the Lord might be telling us through our dreams, we may cast off restraint and suffer the consequences. "Where there is no prophetic vision the people cast off restraint," (Proverbs 29:18).

Riffel warns people not to ignore the voice of God. "God might get their attention through pain by throwing them on a bed of suffering, so they can't stand the sight of food and have no appetite for their favorite treats. They lose weight, wasting away to nothing, reduced to a bag of bones. They hang on the cliff-edge of death, knowing the next breath may be their last" (see Job 33:19-22). Many of us have gone through this, and for me personally, it happened right before I surrendered my life to Christ and started going back to church. One person said, "If you ignore the nudge or whisper from God, the smack will come. If that doesn't get your attention, watch out for the Mack truck heading your way!"

Prognostic

Herman Riffel said, "I see most dreams as diagnostic or prognostic rather than prophetic. The prognosis of a doctor is 'a forecast of the probable course of the disease' (Random House College Dictionary). That forecast is made on the basis of the way that disease has progressed in many other circumstances. It does not say that this will happen, but it is the probable course of the disease. However, prophecy is defined as supernatural, a gift of the Spirit which must be discerned by the Holy Spirit."

"The Bible has two excellent illustrations of the prognostic and the prophetic dreams. Nebuchadnezzar's dream (Daniel 4) of the tree that was cut down which Daniel interpreted to mean that the tree represented him, the king of Babylon. Then Daniel said to the king, 'Renounce your sins by doing right—it may be that then your prosperity will continue'. The prognosis was—you will make it if you repent."

"The prophetic dream, however, is different. It gives a supernatural message from God concerning the future. In Nebuchadnezzar's dream (Daniel 2) about the great statue that was crushed by the rock cut out of the mountain, Daniel interpreted the statue to represent the king, but the rock cut out of the mountain without hands crushes it. Then there is no word saying that if the king repents this will not happen. Instead God gives a prophecy revealing the future, telling what will happen regardless of the action of the king. Through the ages God has given great prophecies, some of which have been about nations. Others are of daily events, but of all the dreams the proportion of prophecy dreams, I believe, are very small."

I have had many dreams that have showed me the events for the day, and many times I only understand the dream as events unfold or after the fact, but I do believe the Lord is trying to show me something through these dreams. Some of them help me avert a disaster (like blowing up in anger), others just show me that God is there and in control (like when He showed me the help He would provide in a job interview).

God wants you to understand what is in your heart and what is going to happen (paraphrase of Daniel 2:29-30). Is it possible that Nebuchadnezzar, much like us, woke up disturbed by his dream but couldn't remember the dream, and that is why he asked them to tell him what his dream was in addition to what it meant? We must look to the Holy Spirit not only for the meaning of a dream but also for help in remembering a dream.

Word of Correction

I have frequent dreams that are prognostic. They tell me what's going to happen that day but also include a word of correction. For example, in 2009, one morning I had this dream:

A female police officer was sitting across from me, and she had a big file folder full of evidence of a crime. She wanted me to make a statement of guilt or innocence. I knew I had done the crime, but I kept silent and fearful of the consequences. She told me it would be better if I made some kind of statement than none at all, otherwise the outcome would be even harder on me. I still kept quiet, fearful of the consequences.

Later that morning we were sitting with our kids at school while they ate breakfast, and one of our neighbors sat next to us. Her kids frequently play with our kids. She said her son was out sick today because he had a cough and a fever. Well, our son also had a cough and a fever last week, and her son frequently comes over and knocks on the door to play. We turned him down several times because our son was sick but eventually let them play together.

While I was sitting there at breakfast, I was feeling guilty that he probably got sick from my son and felt I should apologize but ended up not saying anything—just like in my dream! Obviously, it would have been better if I would have just 'fessed up. This dream also demonstrates that God has a sense of humor too!

Anger Correction Dream

American culture might frown on a word of correction, but God doesn't hesitate to show us, through our dreams, our behavior that needs correction. If we heed His warnings He is faithful to protect us from the consequences.

I had two different dreams (two years apart) where the Lord warned me about my anger. In one situation I managed to avoid getting angry, but in the other I didn't and suffered the consequences.

I had a dream that my wife and I were staying over at my mother's house, and my stepfather was mad at me for coming home late. He was totally in my face, and it felt as if he was overreacting. He said I came home at 4 a.m., and I said it was 1 a.m., maybe 2 a.m. It felt like he was attacking me for some other previously built up frustrations, and it was coming out through this argument. After that, I had another dream where I lost my ID off the lanyard around my neck, but it wasn't a big deal or anything.

That day I went to work, and as soon as I went into the computer lab I was told to switch some of the kids out of the room because they had been in there a long time. According to the sign-in sheet one kid had been in there a long time, and I told him he had to switch rooms. He objected and said he had just come in. I showed him the sign-in sheet, and he said he had forgotten to sign in again after he had come back. I told him the rule was if you don't sign in you get switched out first. He got angry and threw a fit as he walked out the door, so I told him not to come in again that day.

I had many problems with this kid in the past (like the previous built up frustrations in my dream) that caused me to be unbending with him and lay down the law. He brought in another teacher, and she tried to tell me he really did just come in, but I explained to her that didn't matter because of the way he left the room. Then as I walked across the room, she handed me my name tag that had fallen out of my lanyard around my neck that was laying on the floor unbeknownst to me.

At that point, I remembered my dream from that morning where I had lost my ID, and I asked God what was He trying to tell me? A minute later the child brought in the Assistant Director, and she asked about the incident. I explained to her that the level of trust with this kid was at a zero level, and that he threw a fit so he was out for the day.

The Lord was showing me with this dream that I was overreacting and holding onto past resentment, and my built up frustration with this kid was coming out. Losing my name tag was a non-issue because I had another identical one in the closet, but it served as a very clear signal indicating the situation the Lord wanted me to be aware of.

One person commented, "There is no mistaking that your dream was a 'word of correction' from God. All the details line up. Your stepfather was an authority figure in your dream, just as you were the authority figure over the boy in question. There was a dispute pertaining to time in your dream, just as what actually happened that day. You lost your nametag just as you had lost your ID in your dream. I think that God was using this tangible object to remove all doubt that He had given you this dream."

"I think that sometimes we are tempted to pass off our dreams as coincidence or our own imaginations working overtime. When He gives us these undisputable details, we simply cannot shrug off our dream as coming from God since we have no power within ourselves to know the future."

Through this dream, the Lord was telling me that I still need to administer grace, be patient and long suffering both with this child and the authority over me. My step-father is a nice guy, so the Lord was showing me that overreacting was an unusual behavior for myself. We all stumble and fail, but the Lord is there with us and growing us through it.

"We should not be so afraid of the label of hypocrite that we stand still in Christian life, hiding our faith and making no attempts to grow. A person who tries to do right, but often fails is not a hypocrite. A hypocrite is a person who puts on religious behavior in order to gain attention, approval, or admiration from others." (Life Application Study Bible - Luke 6:42).

This dream was the Lord trying to protect me from the enemy's attacks, because on the following Monday the Assistant Director pulled some passive aggressive stuff that was obviously a reaction to our interaction on Friday. If I had backed off I could have avoided this consequence. God's timing was miraculous. He opened my eyes to understand this dream the very minute before she walked in the door. If I only could have averted my anger in time—like I did in the next dream.

Anger Warning Dream

In 2009, I had a dream that was a warning to not blow my top at work, but I didn't understand the meaning of the dream until the exact moment that day when I was about to get angry. Here is the dream:

I was in a hospital, drugged and about to have surgery. I just wanted to rest and crawl under the table. People were asking me why I was angry at the hospital people/nurses. I throw a huge glass brandy snifter over their heads and it smashes on a reception desk, and there are shards everywhere. No one got hit, but they're mad and trying to avoid the shards. I'm wondering if I'm gonna have to go to jail.

I couldn't figure out what the brandy glass meant in the dream, but I knew it was a warning to not get angry, so I reminded myself to keep that in mind during the day. At the end of the work day I sent a kid to tell my coworker I needed someone to come and take over the floor because I was closing the computer lab. The kid came back and told me they said the floor wasn't open. My coworker knew my shift was over but chose to be antagonistic instead of helpful.

I sent another kid, and finally my coworker said to send them to the homework room.

I was very angry at the moment, and I headed across the floor to go upstairs and tell off my coworker, Brandi, for standing around at the front desk talking to the receptionist while I needed someone on the floor. Then it hit me! I was supposed to be careful of my anger! It all fell into place. The huge brandy snifter I threw at the receptionist desk was about my coworker named Brandi. All that morning I was thinking my dream had something to do with alcohol—she hadn't even crossed my mind. The Lord made me forgetful until that very moment. It gave me a little shock when I realized what my dream was about, and it completely threw me out of my anger. I just went, "Wow! That's what my dream was about!" I wasn't angry anymore. I felt like I had God on my side, and I went back to the computer lab and closed up.

One person commented, "It is amazing how the Lord speaks to you frequently in your daily life! The reception desk in your dream clearly foreshadows Brandi standing at the reception desk idly visiting with the receptionist. Wanting to get under a table and rest in your dream symbolized your desire to close the computer lab. I am guessing that there are tables in the lab? The shards of glass represented the sharp words of anger that you almost spoke until you discerned that the dream you had received foretold of that day's events. These sharp words would have caused hard feelings and made your coworker "mad." Your fear of going to jail represented the guilt feelings that you would have had if you had given into your anger that day."

Lastly, through this dream God was telling me that my workplace was a hospital where He was doing surgery on me, and that was why I felt so numb that day and couldn't do much—such as socialize with my coworkers—except for one Christian coworker named John. I felt like God sent John in to talk with me in the computer lab twice that day just to strengthen me.

Comfort Dream

In 2012, the following dream gave me comfort in adjusting to a new workplace situation:

In my dream I am holding a cup, something that I brought in with me from a previous get-together. We're at a bar in front of a club, and a female bartender is trying to sell me an oversized blue martini. It's fancy and expensive and I don't want to buy it, and I also feel I can't afford it. The drink I am holding is half full but still passable as a drink that I'm still working on. I'm thinking their expectation is that you should buy the martini before going in the club but I'm still going in, and it looks like no one is going to stop me.

A cup symbolizes God's will for us or our lot in life. Jesus prayed to have God remove 'this cup' before He was crucified (see Luke 22:41-42). The cup I was holding in my dream was a glass banquet water cup. The week before at a National Prayer Luncheon I had drunk punch out of a similar cup. "A primary Old Testament symbol for the kingdom of God was a banquet table". The banquet cup symbolizes my Christian values—as opposed to a nightlife set of values symbolized by the martini and club.

The martini is James Bond's drink which is "shaken not stirred". Bond is a symbol of spy games, espionage, conspiracy, sex and intrigue. For me these correlated with the values at work. For example, spy games was the gossip mill and espionage was managers who shared with their cohorts confidential information from meetings and emails; and conspiracy, intrigue, and sex related to all of the drama and sexual/sexist jokes. These were common behaviors I had to deal with when I was working for the Army. As one person put it, "working for the DOD was like going back to high school."

The day I had this dream, I went to a coworker's going away party. My drink, in my dream, had some ice in it, and I think it was non-alcoholic, nothing fancy. The one they were trying to sell me was a blue martini. You also find blue in tropical drinks because it's a symbol of relief from worry, calmness and tranquility. I love the tropics, and I don't like confrontation, and if I accept the martini cup of values I would have greater peace at work, but I refuse to do that in my dream because it's too high of a cost. Besides, just like in my dream, I think I can make my way into the club still holding onto my Christian values. A couple weeks before this dream a Christian co-worker was drinking an oversized blue martini (like the one in my dream) at his going away party. He was a great example of dealing with the martini values in the workplace and still being a faithful, loving Christian.

One person commented, "In your dream, the cup you brought with you from a previous get-together symbolizes the Christian values that you bring with you wherever you go. You are not swayed by others ("don't want to buy it") no matter what they are trying to "sell" you or how they try to influence you. When God tells you in your dream that you "can't afford it", I believe He is saying that you can't afford to risk your Christian principles and fellowship with Him to conform to corrupt worldly ways, even though people throughout your life will sometimes expect that conformity. You are "still going in" (functioning well in your workplace, also claiming your eternal inheritance in Heaven), and no one nor any spiritual enemy can stop you. They may try to "shake" you from your position or drag you down to their level, but they can't "stir" you from your iron-clad convictions."

A week after my dream, there was another going away party, and the head of our division gave one of the chiefs a gift of a redneck martini glass (one with a canning jar lid that you can't spill out of). When this happened I knew the Lord was confirming to me the interpretation of my dream. I had never heard anyone talk about martinis in my workplace other than this time and when I saw the blue martini.

One person commented, "I liked your blue martini dream. I have a lot of similar dreams like that, but it's usually where I'm at a gathering where people are eating all sorts of junk foods, and I abstain from the unhealthy choices others are indulging in."

"The Lord is my chosen portion and my cup; you hold my lot" Psalm 16:5.

Pronostic or Prophetic?

The prophets mixed their prognosis and words of correction with their prophecies (both near and distant ones). God does the same with our dreams. He gives us prognostic dreams sometimes and prophetic ones other times.

He frequently shows me things that will happen that day. During times of hardship this happens at least once a week if not more. Many times it's not prognostic, He just shows me what will happen that day. It also seems to have increased as I have dropped using dream dictionaries and begun listening and understanding more.

For example, I had a dream where I was trying to start my wife's/ our car several times, and it wouldn't start. In the dream, we also had an older van that someone had stolen the tires off one side, and the axles were sticking out. I was thinking we were going to have to figure out how to fix that too.

That morning I told my wife about my dream and wondered if it was one of our cars that we were taking in that week and the next week for some warranty work on the air bags. I had also put some oil and water in my car and wondered if I might have put too much water in and if that might effect the running of the car. So we had these things going on that might have been the obvious interpretation of the dream. (However, looking back nothing happened with our cars, and everything went well with the warranty fixes.)

That day, I felt led to spend some quality time with my son, so we spent a couple hours building and programming his Lego robot. At one point I had the tractor track and wheels off of both sides because we needed to pull it apart to replace the batteries. It took quite a bit of effort to put it back together and to put the tractor tracks and wheels on their axles. After that we were having trouble with the programming, and we couldn't get it moving. After several attempts and wondering if we were going to be able to do it, we finally got the programming right, and it turned out awesome!

Maybe the Lord wanted to tell me through this dream to persevere? But I didn't understand the dream until after we had finished, so could it only have been seen as prophetic? If that's the case, I have had more prophetic dreams or just as many as prognostic but haven't kept count.

7

Prophecy

"Follow the way of love and eagerly desire gifts of the Spirit, especially prophecy" (1 Cor. 14:1).

People in our western culture have difficulty with subjective and supernatural experiences and tend to reject feeling or emotion over logic and reason. In the U.S., one in five Christians don't believe in miracles—but in the world, only one out of a thousand Christians don't believe in miracles. One American theologian commented that the Biblical history he was taught in seminary was bereft of miracles but admitted the truth is that our history is filled with miraculous manifestations of the Holy Spirit.

Western culture is not as receptive to the prophetic, for example, the English version of the Bible has the prophets at the end of the Old Testament, but the original Hebrew version has them spread throughout. Our western culture focuses on the facts and history in the Bible and relegates the prophets to the back of the book. The cessationist view, that the spiritual gift of prophecy no longer exists, is a product of Western theology.

It has been my experience, and that of others, the Lord sometimes foretells events in our dreams, and it has nothing to do with being "psychic" but has everything to do with the way the Lord speaks to us. One person commented, "It seems that this is the ultimate reason for our prophetic dreams. I have learned things about our glorious Father through my dreams and leadings: He wants us to pray to Him, He cares about even the smallest details of our lives, He knows our deepest spiritual pain and wants to assure us that He is the Living Water, and through Him all our needs are met. Heaven is real, and we thirst for nothing in His kingdom. He knows beforehand the exact hour of our departure from this earth and every event that will ever take place before it happens. If we pray to Him for forgiveness, He will grant us forgiveness. His compassion is beyond measure."

"Would I have known these things without the dreams? All I can say is that there is a vast difference between reading the words and FEELING their meanings. Prophetic dreams can be like layers of an onion. Peel away one layer of meaning, and beneath that one there is another layer and another. The dreams are not like one sentence written on a piece of paper, or even a paragraph or chapter. Our Creator can give us an entire book with just one brief dream through images, messages, and feelings combined. The more vivid my dream, the more significant it has proven to be."

"Believe in the LORD your God, and you will be established; believe his prophets, and you will succeed" (2 Chronicles 20:20).

Gift of Prophecy

"For you can all prophesy one by one, so that all may learn and all may be exhorted" (1 Cor. 14:31).

Do we all have the gift of prophecy? I suppose it's like the gift of faith. Everyone is supposed to have faith, but some are given a special gifting of faith to benefit the church. For example, taking risks, making leaps of faith, and trusting in God where others may fear to go, and holding onto hope that a particular person will come to Christ.

In a nutshell "A prophet is someone who tells people how God wants them to live, as well as what will happen in the future" (Adventure Bible). God used (and uses) prophets for many functions—but some in certain areas more than others. For example:

Joseph and Daniel were powerful witnesses to others through interpretation of dreams. Isaiah gave incredible prophecies about the Messiah, and John the Baptist proclaimed the Messiah's coming. Isaiah, Daniel, Zechariah, Paul, and the Apostle John prophesied the End Times. He used Samuel, Elijah and Elisha for rebuking and anointing kings. God used Moses, Elijah, Elisha, and Daniel to perform many great miracles. He didn't use Jeremiah for anointing kings or performing miracles but instead for rebuking nations, and to prophesy the destruction of Israel and the return from exile.

He used Joseph, Jeremiah, and Paul for miraculous endurance in the face of persecution. Elijah ran from the death threats of Jezebel. Jeremiah told the people they can do what they want, but if they killed him innocent blood would be on their heads. And Paul said I would rather be with the Lord, but it is better for me to be here for your benefit.

Hosea, Joel, and Malachi rebuked Israel. Habakkuk and Amos prophesied Israel's destruction. Jonah and Nahum called the people of Nineveh (Assyria) to repent. Zephaniah warned Israel and other nations. Obadiah prophesied that Israel's enemies will be punished. And God used Paul and the Apostle John to rebuke and encourage churches.

"See, today I appoint you over nations and kingdoms to uproot and tear down, to destroy and overthrow, to build and to plant" (Jeremiah 1:10).

"who through faith conquered kingdoms, enforced justice, obtained promises, stopped the mouths of lions" (Hebrews 11:33).

And Jesus did all of these things. He performed miracles and called everyone to repentance. He rebuked religious and political leaders, prophesied near and future events, and the End Times.

Testing the Gift of Prophecy

There are several tests for a prophet. What he or she says must line up with the Word of God: "If anyone thinks he is a prophet or spiritual, let him recognize that the things which I write to you are the Lord's commandment. But if anyone does not recognize this, he is not recognized." (1 Cor. 14:37)

A prophet is to be self-controlled, and other prophets are to judge what they say: "And the spirits of prophets are subject to prophets" (1 Cor. 14:32). "Let the prophets speak two or three, and let the other judge" (1 Corinthians 14:29).

False prophecy should be taken as seriously as false doctrine in the church: "But there were also false prophets among the people, just as there will be false teachers among you. They will secretly introduce destructive heresies," (2 Peter 2:1).

Another test for prophets is whether their predictions come true: "As for the prophet who prophesies peace, when the word of that prophet comes to pass, then it will be known that the LORD has truly sent the prophet" (Jeremiah 28:9).

There are people making prophecies and interpreting dreams that have given these gifts a bad name. One person commented, "That is why I am reluctant to divulge my dreams to anyone. I've often wondered how many have these dreams. Perhaps more than we know. With all the skepticism in the world, they may be reluctant to share it."

One author involved in prophetic ministry tested dream interpretations from several Christian prophetic ministries. They were all offered the same dream to interpret and no one came up with the same interpretation, and some even said they had confirmation from the Lord. This prophetic author commented, "Perhaps many of our dreams are not meant to be interpreted by others, but for us to press into God until we get an understanding of what He is saying."

We can see in the Bible that some believers (Joseph and Daniel) helped non-believers understand their dreams. This makes sense since non-believers haven't learned to hear the voice of God. However, believers need to learn how to hear the voice of God in all parts of their life and understand that God speaks to all of us in the riddles of our dreams.

Cessationism

Cessationism is a theological theory that rejects prophecy, among other things, and is taught at many American seminaries and Christian colleges. In 2012, one theologian who worked for Rocky Mountain Bible College & Seminary was asked to resign after he realized (and shared with his employer) that cessationism is a theory that has absolutely no Biblical evidence. "The particular instance of cessationism that led to my resignation was RMBC&S's teaching statement on the issue, which reads, 'The miraculous gifts (apostles, prophets, healings, miracles including a word of wisdom or word of knowledge, and tongues) were temporary in nature as signs to unbelieving Jews and as a validation of the New Testament message and its messengers at the initial stage of the church'" (fullcontactchristianity.org).

The cessationists are like the Sadducees who neither interpreted scripture correctly nor understood the power of God. "Jesus said to them, "Is this not the reason you are wrong, because you know neither the Scriptures nor the power of God?" (Mark 12:24).

Cessationists deny the authority of scripture

Cessationists deny the authority of scripture by placing their theological theories over God's Word. Cessationists invalidate scripture in Acts, 1 Corinthians, Ephesians,

Hebrews and other books of the Bible. Paul wrote many books of the Bible that contain scriptures that the cessationists reject and twist. Peter's words are appropriate for the cessationists: "Paul also wrote to you according to the wisdom given him, as he does in all his letters when he speaks in them of these matters. There are some things in them that are hard to understand, which the ignorant and unstable twist to their own destruction, as they do the other Scriptures" (2 Peter 3:15-16).

Cessationists claim the spiritual gift of prophecy is simply preaching and that the office of prophet no longer exists: "And he gave the apostles, the prophets, the evangelists, the shepherds and teachers" (Eph. 4:11). However, the word prophet is used in association with the spiritual gift of prophecy in 1 Cor. 12. We can also see from the following description that a prophet (someone with the gift of prophecy) is very different from the gift of teaching or preaching:

"The true prophet is conscious of being called to declare, not the results of his own investigations or reflections, but the counsels and will of the Most High. He utters the word of God. It may be a message that runs counter to his own preference, that excites the deepest grief in his soul, that overcomes him with surprise and terror; but he cannot keep silent...he distinguishes between his own thoughts and words and the word of God...The truth which he pours forth from a soul exalted, yet not confused by emotion is not something reasoned out. It is an immediate perception of intuition. He is a seer: he hears or beholds that which his tongue declares" (The Grounds of Theistic and Christian Belief, pub. 1915). (This is from a book that my great-grandfather had who was a Methodist minister 100 years ago.)

Cessatanism

Cessationists deny that the Holy Spirit works through believers with gifts like prophecy and apostleship. They mislead people to believe their spiritual gift isn't real or from the enemy. They cut off half of the spiritual gifts in the church leaving an anemic or spiritually dead body of Christ. They deny youth and adults the chance to learn about their spiritual gifts and develop them.

One person commented cessationism is, "a doctrine that puts God in a box and strips Him of His power. Jesus' hometown didn't believe Him, and as a result He could do no miracle there except that He laid His hands on a few sick people and healed them (Mark 6:1-6). I think of all the blessings that the people in Jesus' hometown missed out on, and how people today miss the many blessings that could be theirs because of the same limitation they put on Him."

Cessatanism (as I now call it) is a philosophy that empowers the enemy, disempowers believers, and denies the work of the Holy Spirit. Cessatanists place more faith in people being used by demons than by the Holy Spirit. They believe the demonic acts displayed in the book of Acts are possible today, but they don't believe the prophetic acts (such as foretelling) displayed in the book of Acts are possible today.

Cessatanists are quick to judge a word from the Lord as false prophecy or satanic, and dreams as demonic. "In order to compass their own selfish ends, simply because they felt His life and teaching would interfere with them, they dared to ascribe to the devil what their own hearts told them came direct from God" (Pulpit Commentary).

"Here it is a word of encouragement to disciples (apostles) to this effect: blaspheming the Holy Spirit speaking through you will be in God's sight an unpardonable sin, far more heinous than that of prejudiced Pharisees speaking evil against me, the Son of Man, now." (Expositor's Greek Testament).

"And everyone who speaks a word against the Son of Man will be forgiven, but anyone who blasphemes against the Holy Spirit will not be forgiven" (Luke 12:10).

Cessatanism is in the same spirit as evolution. Evolution denies what God has done in the past—whereas cessatanism denies what God is doing today.

"Jesus Christ is the same yesterday and today and forever" (Hebrews 13:8).

Continuationists

There are many people who say they believe the spiritual gifts are for today, but in practice they are no different from the cessationists. 'Open but cautious' is many times a cover for being a cessationist in practice. The cessationists are like the Sadducees who neither interpreted scripture correctly nor understood the power of God. Jesus told us to be wary of the teachings of the Pharisees and Sadducees. Therefore, if someone is truly cessationist in practice, his teachings are something we also need to be 'cautious yet open' about.

A continuationist is someone who believes the spiritual gifts (like prophecy) continue today, but some, like John Piper, are still skeptical. Piper gives an example of someone who prophesied that his fourth baby would be a girl, and his wife would die in childbirth. Both of these were false prophecies because they didn't come true.

Many cessationists (and even continuationists) have had experiences with false premonitions or false prophecies yet fail to realize that prophets need to be trained properly. Prophets, as well as Christians in general, need to be trained in how to hear the Lord through the many ways He speaks to us.

There needs to be discipleship and schools for prophets—just like teachers and preachers have. Elijah the prophet spent time discipling Elisha. In several places in the Bible, there is mention of groups of prophets, and some of these groups were led by prophets like Samuel and Elisha. It appears that these were schools for prophets, and some were large groups. During the time of Elisha, the building that held all the prophets that Elisha was in charge of had gotten too small (2 Kings 6:1 ESV).

There is an answer to cessationism, Wayne Grudem commented in an interview posted online, "I think that the first century church and the New Testament generally encourages us to seek miraculous workings of the Holy Spirit much more than we do in mainstream Evangelical churches. I think if we did, and if we taught about spiritual gifts that were consistent with Scripture and which put safeguards against abuses, that we would see a much greater explosion of the powerful working of the Holy Spirit in bringing more unbelievers to Christ and in bringing physical and emotional and relational healing to people within our churches and in bringing us to new levels of joy in worship beyond the very positive things that we see today".

Confirming Dream

I had the following dream during a week when I was confronting church leadership on the false doctrine of cessationism. It matches events that happened the day of the dream and the next day.

In the first segment of the dream, I have to catch a plane and move out of the house. My wife is saying we still have stuff in the house, and I'm saying we have to go and now remember that it's because we sold the house. Most of the things in the house are gone, but there are still a few things like a bookcase with stuff on it. I realize there is nothing we can do at this point, and the new owners will be moving in soon. I tell her we'll just have to pay someone to move this stuff after we go. I'm trying to get her going; I think we have a flight to catch.

This section of the dream was basically what happened the morning of the dream. My wife and I were talking about and worried about having to move to another church because I had confronted the church leadership on their false doctrine of cessationism. My wife obviously didn't want to leave because like in the dream we still have stuff we own there, that is to say, an investment of ourselves in the church of friends, membership, etc. In the dream I am thinking that there isn't much we can do at this time. We can't change the situation.

In the next segment of the dream, I'm at a hotel and going to catch a flight and had some of my brother's long plaid shorts on. He was staying in the hotel room and wasn't leaving like I was. I took off the plaid shorts, and someone else took off a pair of red, thick corduroy short pants and put on the plaid shorts. That isn't what I had in mind. I realized I didn't have anything else to put on and wanted to put back on the plaid ones, but now, because I had to go, I had put on the red corduroy ones even though they were pretty ugly.

Just like in the first dream segment there is a feeling of leaving (and for the same reasons). My brother is a logical minded fellow, and our church leaders were fairly logical and intellectual, so I had to put on that mindset in order to speak their language when I conversed with or confronted them. The plaid shorts symbolize my casual attitude that has now changed to one symbolized by the red short pants. I wanted to go back to being casual, but now that I had confronted leadership I couldn't. My wife also suggested the short pants symbolize falling short. We all fall short of the glory of God, myself included, so no matter how I approached the issue I wasn't going to be perfect.

My wife had commented that the pants style was from the 80s. At the men's Bible study the next day I brought up the topic of spiritual gifts and asked the church's position. The Bible study leader didn't answer and thought this debate had died out some time ago, but evidently was still alive today. Apparently, it was a hot topic back in the 70s and 80s, so my wearing those ugly thick corduroy short pants was symbolic of bringing back up an old ugly topic from the past, and the red symbolizing my passion on the topic.

In the last segment of the dream, I'm at a small group with four or five other guys, and there is a lady hosting it who gave a bowl of corn to pass around. The facilitator asked a question for everyone to answer, something like, what was their favorite part of Christianity?

The first guy answered and summed up exactly my own thoughts. I'm third in line to answer the question, but I jump in and say I think the same thing (as the first guy). They ask me my answer, and I can't exactly remember what the first guy said. I try to explain it in my own words, that it's like being under an umbrella of the Lord. Then, I have munched quite a bit of corn and thought the bowl was finished, but it is full again so it must have been refilled, and I'm feeling too full.

There was a lady who hosted the men's Bible study (like in my dream) at her house, and there was always something to eat. These facts tipped me off that this was what the dream was about. I guessed the corn symbolized a bowl of popcorn being passed around—however, they never had snacks like popcorn, so I wasn't sure.

The Lord revealed that there would be something said that struck a chord in me. And there was! The Bible study leader said that if we look at the Greek word for 'perfect' in 1 Corinthians 13:10, it is actually plural, so that invalidates the cessationists argument that the perfect came (and the end of the spiritual gifts) with the closing of the canon of the Bible. I said, "Exactly!" It was just like in my dream: he summed it up better than I could. Later he told me that he grew up in the Baptist tradition, which was cessationist, but now believes that God can do anything. This was the 'umbrella statement' in my dream.

The next morning (before this Bible study) I had another dream:

I was sitting at what seemed like kind of a Home Depot workshop with a bunch of older Asian ladies. I feel a little out of place, and they begin to discuss a previous page in a book we have in front of us. In the book is a photo and list of a bunch of healthy food. I want to say I don't care for any of it but instead try to find something I like in the list. I find a couple items like lettuce that I guess are okay.

After having this dream I guessed from the feelings in the dream, and the group of older Asians, that it was about the Bible study that night because most of the members were older Asian guys. After the Bible study we adjourned to the dining room for cakes and conversation, kind of like you would see a group of ladies do (just like in my dream).

One of the guys wasn't eating anything and spent quite a bit of time discussing his ideas on healthy eating (like the book in my dream). I didn't really care to talk about it (like in my dream). However, as we were leaving, he told one of the men that he has tried to cut out all high fructose foods. I mentioned that my glucose has been high at times and have to watch it. They mentioned another member who was pre-diabetic but is now diabetic. At that point, I was regretting having eaten that second chocolate éclair because my glucose has also been pre-diabetic at times.

Later that night when I thought more about the dream and talked to my wife, she mentioned that high fructose is associated with corn syrup. In the last segment of my dream from the previous day, there was a bowl of cut corn (like out of a can). In my dream I had already eaten some, and they had refilled the bowl but I was already feeling full and feeling bad about how much I had already eaten.

The high fructose conversation—symbolized by a bowl of cut corn in my dream—was something I never could have imagined. Through these two dreams the Lord showed me everything would turn out all right—at a time when I feared what would happen after I confronted the church leadership about their false doctrine of cessationism.

It also was a confirmation that I heard Him correctly in the word from Him that I gave to the leadership, because He surely would have given me a warning or correction dream if my actions were wrong—like He has done in the past—but instead He gave me a dream comforting me and assuring me. He told me what would happen so that I wouldn't fear, and that there would be a bright spot in the Bible study where someone would speak my very thoughts!

I probably wouldn't have made it to that Bible study if it hadn't been for that affirmation from my dream. I was feeling spiritually stretched and didn't have the energy to go. Right after I arrived one of the members gave me the word that we will never 'feel' equipped. The key is whether the Lord is telling us to do something or not, and being obedient to that, and disregard not feeling up to it, or doubting our abilities and strength.

I wouldn't have made it to Bible study without this affirming dream.

8

Prophetic Dreams

"I am the LORD; that is my name! I will not give my glory to anyone else. I will not share my praise with carved idols. Everything I prophesied has come true, and now I will prophesy again. I will tell you the future before it happens" (Isaiah 42:8-9).

Jesus gave many prophecies that happened the same day, within a year or two, and in the distant future. In the New Testament (after Pentecost) both Agabus and Paul demonstrated the prophetic gift when they foretold events. Agabus foretold Paul's imprisonment, and Paul foretold that a boat voyage to Rome would end in disaster and that they would all die.

In Jeremiah chapter thirty-two, Jeremiah receives a prophecy (probably through a vision or dream) that his cousin is coming to sell his field to him and then, right after that, it comes true. From that Jeremiah knew that it was God's will for him to purchase the land from his cousin.

"Jeremiah said, "The word of the Lord came to me: Behold, Hanamel the son of Shallum your uncle

will come to you and say, 'Buy my field that is at
Anathoth, for the right of redemption by purchase
is yours.' Then Hanamel my cousin came to me in
the court of the guard, in accordance with the word
of the Lord, and said to me, 'Buy my field that is
at Anathoth in the land of Benjamin, for the right
of possession and redemption is yours; buy it for
yourself.' Then I knew that this was the word of the
Lord" (Jeremiah 32:6-8 ESV).

I have had prophetic dreams that were simply the Lord
'telling me the future before it happens', showing me what
He was going to do or what would come to pass, and like
Jeremiah, 'I knew that this was the word of the Lord'. In one
dream the Lord showed me that I would change my workplace
a year and a half later. In another dream He showed us a
rental apartment that He would give us nine months later.
In the first case, I understood that something was going to
happen a year and a half later, but in the second case the
Lord didn't show me the meaning until a month after we got
the apartment, and I stumbled on the dream in my journal
(while researching for this book).

Job Change Dream

On April 20th, 2008 I had the following dream which
was fulfilled one and a half years later:

*I'm walking back to our old apartment (not one from real life).
It's the end of April and it will be turned over to new renters in a
few days, but I still have the key because I'm still paying rent. The
complex has changed, it has gotten worse. Along the street are tons
of people's stuff and lots of bikes filling up half the street so that*

cars have to go halfway up the curb to pass. I am on-foot and walk through the complex towards the apartment. There are lots of things on the lawn, sort of obstacles. There are some trashy, little-bit-scary looking people everywhere that weren't living there when we were there. I was glad I didn't live here with the kids anymore and was happy about our new apartment that was at a completely different place not in this complex.

I approach the building and more kinda scary looking people, and I pretend not to notice them and act like I belong there. I make my way up the stairs (it's on the third or fourth floor), and on the way up I run into two of my old neighbors that I was friendly with. One guy, probably my age, isn't bothered by the people at the complex getting worse. The other guy is older and wants to move out, but is living here for his job convenience. He has a year and a half until retirement, and then he won't have to live here anymore. He said he could move out, but the options would be living in the Bronx, and that wouldn't be any improvement. I told him you can hold your breath for only a year and a half until retirement. He questioned that. I said look at the military guys, they do it all the time to finish up their commitment with the military. He still seemed like it was too much of a burden for him, but he didn't know what else to do.

The old guy in the dream wasn't anyone I knew in real life, so he didn't symbolize anything to me other than a federal job. A month before the dream, I started applying for federal jobs, and I figured this dream was God telling me that I would get a federal job (which turned out to be true).

Nine days before this dream I applied for a computer teacher job with the Army which included a background investigation and a year probation, so I figured that was what the year and a half from my dream symbolized. I had an interview and subsequent job offer two weeks after this dream. I started work two months after the dream. My wife and I wondered what God planned to do in a year and a half, and we kept this dream in mind.

The place where I got the job was considered the worst youth center, with all kinds of problems with the kids, employee turnover, and shortage of staff. After I started the job I realized that this was the 'bad neighborhood' in my dream. I had to commute (like the guy in my dream), and we couldn't move closer to work because my kid's school would be in the Bronx per se.

There were many obstacles (like in my dream) to overcome. There were tons of boxes of junk that had to be cleaned out of the computer lab, and piles of junk and old computers in other storage closets in the center (symbolized by all the people's stuff in my dream). The computer room closet was filled with bikes (like my dream). We took the bikes out, and there was an uncovered hole where a toilet used to be and hundreds of cockroaches. The trashy, scary people in my dream were some of the coworkers and management who were the most unprofessional people I have ever worked with. It took me several years to understand that the Army as a whole was an extremely toxic workplace.

One day (10-20-09) everyone was called into work early for a staff meeting with the bosses' boss. That morning, before going to work, I listened to a sermon on Joseph's life. Joseph told the cupbearer that the three branches in his dream meant in three days he would be raised up out of prison and restored to his position. The cupbearer's dream was fulfilled three days after he had the dream. I had been thinking that maybe today was the day that God would fulfill my dream since it was exactly a year and a half after my dream—to the day! But I wasn't sure, because it could also be December 20th, which was a year and a half after I started work.

I went into work early and my bosses' boss took me into the office and offered me a transfer to a different youth center. All I could say was, "Hallelujah and Praise God". I felt like the cupbearer, who Joseph told would be raised up out of prison, when I was taken out of this youth center and transferred to a better, closer one. I had applied for several jobs at the new location, yet, on the day the Lord determined, they finally offered it to me as a transfer.

Lastly, the military comment in my dream foreshadowed that I would be working for the Army. In terms of retirement (in the dream) I did end up working for the Army long enough (over six years) to be eligible to receive a small pension when I retire, although it was like the guy in my dream—I really questioned whether I could survive long enough to qualify for a pension.

Alaska prophecy

Sometimes when I have a dream on a Sunday morning it will be about something that coming week, just like when the Lord speaks into my week through the Sunday sermon. It's not about omens or signs, it's about the Lord giving us a heads up.

My wife and I both had dreams on the same night (a Monday morning) of it snowing in Hawaii. This happened two days before a series of events took place that led us to move from Hawaii to Alaska.

On Monday the 17th of January, 2011, I had a dream that I was talking on the phone to an old college buddy that lives in Colorado, and he said there was lots of snow in Colorado. I said, "Yes, I had heard that, but now they had gotten even more." And then I told him, "We are getting snow in Hawaii too!" I looked out the window and told him it was only a quarter inch or so (but maybe really looked like an inch?) It was snowing lightly, and I wanted to hurry and take a picture before it stopped snowing and started melting, so I could email a picture to him and others.

That same morning my wife had this dream:

She had a scary dream where some guy she didn't know had killed a shark. She and a group of people were trying to help cover it up because someone was trying to catch him? She was trying to bury in the sand the shovel that he used to kill it, and there were shark bones.

Then she was in a sort of high-rise building (like the mansions you have in Japan), but it was Hawaii. She was looking outside. It was snowing, and she was telling our daughter to look quick because it was starting to rain and melt away.

A day or two before I had my dream I had spoken on the phone with an old college buddy (a different one from the one in the dream). We had talked about his government career and the number of years he had spent in it before he transitioned out to a new career working for a large corporation. In my dream there were two layers of heavy snow in Colorado. The first symbolized his accumulated years in the government, and the next layer was his current career in the private sector ("they have gotten even more").

The snow in both of our dreams was a surprise and completely unexpected (as it would be if it snowed in Hawaii). Two days later, I received an email stating I made the referral list for a job in Alaska. I didn't want to go to Alaska, but I figured that I would apply for everything I could—especially since the job market was so bad—and see where the Lord opened the door. "We may cast lots, but the Lord determines how they fall" (Proverbs 16:33). "Even the events that seem accidental are really ordered by Him" (Amplified Bible). I had applied for this Alaska job and many others a couple months before, so making the list on the 19th and getting a phone call on the 20th was completely out of the blue. I interviewed the following Monday, and two days later they asked me to fly out and visit them in Alaska.

Two weeks after our snow dreams, the Lord showed me this verse: "As for having two similar dreams, it means that these events have been decreed by God, and he will soon make them happen" (Genesis 41:32). This is what Joseph told Pharaoh when the Pharaoh had two similar dreams in the same night. In that case, it was one person having two similar dreams, so wouldn't two people having similar dreams the same night be an even greater witness? If it was just about me flying to an interview in Alaska I don't think He would have given my wife the same dream. I think we both had the same dream because the outcome would affect both of us. God had decreed these Alaska events. It was a sign for both of us that foretold our moving to Alaska.

I flew to the interview thinking to myself it would be a chance to get away but not thinking seriously about the job. During the week I spent in Alaska, a government hiring freeze came into effect and lasted about two and a half months. The Lord gave us plenty of time to think it over.

The hiring freeze allowed us time to apply for the lottery to a magnet/charter public school in Alaska for our kids. We were notified in April that our children won the lottery for entrance into that school. In the beginning of June, the hiring freeze ended. I was offered the job, and we prayerfully accepted. Our children were able to finish the school year in Hawaii, and we moved during the summer vacation.

In both of our dreams we were trying to capture the moment because we knew the snow wouldn't last. After our three-year commitment in Alaska was over, we exercised our return rights, per our transportation agreement, and the Lord moved us back (all expenses paid!) to Hawaii.

In Hawaii, a friend from Colorado who lived in Hawaii told us that God brings people to Hawaii to humble them— and it was in Hawaii where my wife and I surrendered our lives to Christ. Another person from Colorado, in a Bible study in Alaska, told me that God brings people to Alaska to grow them. God used our time in Alaska, as one Christian friend pointed out, as a wilderness experience like the Israelites who were in the desert after Egypt, or like Paul who went to Arabia after his conversion. I believe He took us to Alaska (and miraculously brought us back) for that very purpose.

Alaska Dream/Vision

After the job interview on the phone, I flew up to Alaska to meet them. While sleeping in the hotel, I had a dream that seemed like an out of body experience. Although it was winter, there were heavy curtains to keep out the light on the long Alaska summer days so it was very dark in the hotel room. Normally I couldn't see anything, but in this vision I could see the wall and part of the room. There was a heating vent at the top of the wall and that is where I flew through the wall. I woke up thinking I should call my wife and tell her about it, but it was too late at night.

I was flying through the wall of the hotel room, and on the other side was another room, and in that room was a large screen television. In the room there were lots of people. My family was there and in particular my nephew and maybe my brother. Also, on one side were a bunch of Japanese women who were behaving inappropriately.

The Lord didn't show me what this dream meant until we moved back to Hawaii, and I was researching for this book. I was reviewing a dream from May 2008 about a computer teacher interview, and I remembered the dream that I had in the hotel while in Alaska for my job interview.

After we moved to Alaska, we made friends with some Christian families like ours who had American husbands and Japanese wives. I got to be good friends with one of these American husbands. He was symbolized by my nephew in my dream. My nephew studied Japanese and went to Japan to teach English like I did, and mentioned that we tend to think alike. This guy had also lived in Japan and kind of looked like my nephew. We came up with the idea of starting a church together and named it the Japanese Fellowship.

Our town home was part of an association that had a community center. We held our Japanese Fellowship church in the community center every other Sunday. The community center had a big screen television on the wall (like my dream) that I used to display music lyrics while I played the guitar and we worshiped.

Our Japanese Fellowship church actually grew out of a Japanese ladies' Bible study, so there were several Japanese ladies in attendance. There had been some disagreements among the ladies about the teachings and other things, and some stopped attending. These were the ladies in my dream who were acting inappropriately.

In the dream I was flying through the wall and above the room which symbolized soaring to spiritual heights. This fellowship group was probably the best thing that happened to us in the three years we were in Alaska. Even after we returned to Hawaii I had been questioning whether it was God's will that we went to Alaska, but when I finally understood this dream I saw it as a confirmation of His plan.

Apartment prophecy

One of my co-workers pointed out that the Holy Spirit guides us like a compass, and this is something non-believers lack. I love the compass idea, and dreams are also part of that compass. I have found that many of my dreams come in three parts. Many times the first part is telling me what is going right now, then the next part what will happen next, and the third part being the conclusion or outcome of those events.

In September, 2013 in Alaska I had a three part dream about an apartment the Lord planned to give to us when we moved back to Hawaii in June of 2014. He showed me the meaning of the dream after we moved in the apartment.

Don's family (friends of ours in real life who lived in the same townhouse community that we lived in when we live in Hawaii) bought an incredible new house that was shaped like a long greenhouse with lots of windows (kind of like a building we had seen on a British Railways show that was a beautiful historic greenhouse) and with beautiful light shining in and coming in everywhere. I was kind of jealous that he got the perfect house facing the perfect direction for the sun to shine in. The second floor had his kid's rooms and the sun shined in everywhere, and down something like an escalator going to the end of the house was an incredible master bedroom. It was amazing how the light shined in everywhere. The kids seem to have rooms which appear to be without walls.

Next, I'm downstairs in a front area living room on a couch talking to one Don's acquaintances. Don has emails I sent him displayed on a flat screen—emails where I was giving him advice on financing his home. The emails have something like two lines and both say: Leasing: Days and times: Isaiah (10 or 11):6-9.

Next I'm possibly in front of the house, and it might be dark outside and maybe we're around a BBQ. The same guy or another of Don's acquaintances says Don's deal came through the Cub Scouts, and it seems that Sharon's deal did too. Her great deal was on a mortgage rate, but it wasn't clear how they helped Don, maybe with a mortgage rate or some other financial assistance.

The guy telling me about both deals said I needed to belong to a group like that (the Cub Scouts) to get a good deal. I was like, "Yeah, yeah, I know. I've been part of a credit union, and you can get a quarter percent discount on a loan." He replied that Sharon got a zero percent mortgage. I was shocked and surprised. How is that possible? What kind of group is that? The feeling I had in the dream was that Don's deal was almost as good a deal—but Sharon's was the best.

Eight days after we moved back to Hawaii, we were staying in a hotel looking for apartments and one of our friends, who we knew through my son's Cub Scouts, emailed us to tell us he had a rental unit that he hadn't put on the market yet. It was in the same townhouse community we had lived in before, was available immediately, and the rent was below market (*"I needed to belong to a group like that (the Cub Scouts) to get a good deal"*)!

We went and inspected the unit and were surprised to find that it was in the same building as Don's unit. We had previously lived on the opposite side of the community from Don's family but now—just like the Lord intimated in my dream—we now lived in the same building! Since it was a two-bedroom apartment and we have three kids, the baby stayed in the room with us. The kids didn't want to share a room, so my son took part of the living room as his room (*rooms which appear to be without walls*).

God many times uses hyperbole in dreams. Hyperbole is exaggerated statements or claims not meant to be taken literally. In dreams the purpose is to catch your attention and make you remember the dream. Our new apartment wasn't like living in that big beautiful greenhouse on the British Railways show, but it had many of the same feelings for me—I was very happy with the view out the back window onto the park. There was a privacy wall that allowed us to keep our window blinds open, and the sun shined in through the trees. It was a wonderful feeling after living in Alaska!

Two days before I discovered this dream in my journal I stopped by Don's house, and he talked about wanting to sell their house. I told him he should sell in the summer and buy in the winter because prices always go down in the winter, somewhere around 10k (*"advice on financing his home"*). After I talked with Don I started researching the market and found a townhouse for sale in our complex. The price was a lot higher than I imagined. I did some research on home loans and found the Good Neighbor Next Door Federal program that sells foreclosed homes to teachers at half the price.

Then I discovered this dream in my journal and realized it was about our apartment and made the connection with Sharon, a coworker who used to have the same job as me and was a former a teacher. I know from owning houses in the past that the accrued interest on a 30 year mortgage is about equal to the cost of the house. Therefore, "*Sharon getting a zero percent mortgage*" is the same as a teacher paying half the price.

In the second segment of my dream, I couldn't remember if it was Isaiah 10 or 11. The first scripture Isaiah 10:6-9 is about God's future plans of judgment on Assyria, the country God used to destroy Israel because it had turned away from God. The second scripture, Isaiah 11:6-9, is about the coming of the perfect and God's perfect plan. The second scripture spoke to me that very day because we were having a debate in my online Biblical studies course about the coming (*Days and times*) of the 'perfect' in 1 Corinthians 13:10. I felt the Lord was showing me the answer to this discussion— that the perfect is when Isaiah 11:6-9 is fulfilled and the lion (or wolf) lays down next to the lamb.

Lastly, the same week we extended our apartment lease Don put his house on the market (*Leasing: Days and times:*). This dream was fairly recent compared my other prophetic dreams, and I believe that the Lord may reveal more about it as time passes.

Prophetic Dreams About Others

I have a had a couple dreams about my family's lives. I dreamed something about India and my wife, and when I told her the dream she said she was in the middle of reading a travelogue of a Japanese guy who traveled through India. I also had a dream where my daughter's teacher told me she got such a high score on a test that she wanted to retest her, and the next time it was even higher. Then in real life, her GT (gifted and talented) teacher told us that she had taken an IQ test at school, and she said she has never seen a score that high and recommended some summer courses and special summer camps at the university.

As I was writing this book, I was given a prophetic dream pertaining to someone else. In the dream He showed me what was going on in her life, but I wouldn't have known this without her interpreting the dream.

At a farm, a lady is pointing out the trees that line all around the field. She tells me they used to use those trees to post signs on (apparently on every tree around the property, kind of like a no trespassing sign but said something different, something more useful). The trees aren't straight, but more the kind that have trunks that are curved and very thick and hard looking wood. Then we approach the house, and she tells me that the trees were all killed. Now I can see that they aren't live trees. She tells me her husband saw that they were putting down fertilizer that said something else on the bag, (below the fertilizer label something added like seed?) and he told them not to use it because it would harm the trees.

We're inside or in between two buildings, and she indicates the building on the left is where her husband put the bag of fertilizer he told them not to use, but then later the ladies (in the office) used it. Next, we're inside the house/building in a small sort of cashiers office. I'm standing behind a counter behind/next to a cash register talking to her and I say, "Martha it's nice to finally meet you in person". She was a smaller lady than I imagined with a friendly face and a smile. She explains to me that the ladies used the fertilizer bag that her husband had put in the other building and that is what killed all the trees (that border the property).

Martha is walking along the hall with a customer. I'm around the corner standing in the doorway of a small office with a window and a computer sort of like an accounting office talking to one of her employees. Apparently, Martha had told me that she wouldn't let any of the ladies work on something (on the left half of the farm with the cows?) after they used the bad fertilizer, and they could only take care of the chickens now (which are on the right half). The younger lady in the office wasn't happy about the incident and its result, but she also said something like she wouldn't want to work anyplace else and imagined herself working there all the way until retirement. And I'm thinking, or maybe she said, it's something about the friendly, easy, laid-back atmosphere in the office. She told me about her milking a cow(s), and I said I had sorta done it once.

I knew Martha had a father who had an orchard where the trees had been cut down. She commented, "The trees were planted in rows ("line all around the field") on the 10 acres. Could the signs have been the varieties of apple trees? Most of the trees were dwarf with curving branches." I had corresponded by email with Martha, but never met her in person. I described to her what she looked like in the dream (age, height, and weight), and the description actually fit the lady who lived with her father.

Martha commented, "There is a dairy farm that borders one side of my dad's property. As I read about your dream, I am almost freaking out because I was going to say something about fertilizer in my next post to you!" Before I had emailed her this dream, she was composing an email about my high-fructose corn syrup dream (in the chapter on Prophecy). In that email she wrote, "Keep in mind that we grow corn for a living, but here is what is happening. The huge CAFOs (confined animal feeding operations) have pits of several acres containing liquid manure. This e-coli ridden waste must be disposed of in some fashion. So, with the blessing of the Federal Dept. of Agriculture, who stripped all regulatory power from the EPA, this liquid manure is pumped through long draglines into farmers' crop fields. Certain farmers agree to accept it so they reduce their fertilizer costs. When you buy corn syrup, some of the corn that went into it was grown in this way."

This was the bad fertilizer in my dream! I have never heard of CAFOs or liquid manure fertilizer and didn't know she was writing me about that in her next email. She also told me that the neighboring dairy farm had expressed interest in buying her father's property. After further discussion she concluded, "I am getting a stronger feeling that the neighbor will buy it to grow corn for ensilage for his dairy herd...God may have been showing you what I wished could have been: the continuation of the orchard, cash register, employees, and what in reality will happen: seed planted, fertilizer, milk cows."

Dual Meaning

There can be dual meanings of the same dream, i.e. two interpretations for the same part of the dream. For example, in the book of Revelation the Apostle John is given two meanings for 'the seven heads':

"This calls for a mind with wisdom: the seven heads are seven mountains on which the woman is seated;

they are also seven kings, five of whom have fallen, one is, the other has not yet come, and when he does come he must remain only a little while" (Rev. 17:9-10).

One person commented, "I have had dreams that have had a double meaning for the same part, which is what I meant by 'layers of meaning.' He can give us multiple meanings with one image or thought.

The dream I had the morning of my mother's heart attack, as the dream progressed, about half way into the dream, our house began to rise off the ground. I looked down (again from a window) and saw our cat that looked very small below us. Even though the sky was blood red, the ground was rippling like the waves of an ocean, and all was chaotic outside, everything inside was peaceful. Not even one piece of china in the cupboard rattled as we ascended. But, we only ascended about 50 feet into the air, then I awoke.

My original interpretation was that my mother's body was in chaos as she lay unconscious from her heart attack, as shown to me by what was going on outside the house (body). Inside, nothing was touched...all was peaceful. God was keeping her spirit (inside) at peace.

Later I realized the double meaning concerning the ascension of our house. It only ascended part way because the life squad had resuscitated my mother after her heart had stopped, thereby interrupting her ascension to Heaven. Even though the house rising in my dream was the one in which my family lives, my mother was so much a part of me that it was as if my home were also hers. So, the image of the house rising meant that God was lifting us up (in our home) away from the chaotic, rippling earth below, thereby protecting us as we gathered together in our living room to pray, and the same image also meant that my mother's ascension to Heaven was interrupted for the 3 weeks that she was in a coma.

I think that we should keep in mind our dreams and not close the chapter so quickly...perhaps the Lord isn't finished with the story yet."

National Events

I have had very few dreams about others. My dreams are usually about myself and my circumstances. One person commented, "I have had some dreams specifically about me from the Lord, but I think that most often mine are not about myself." She has had dreams about others, premonitions about others she didn't know very well and others close to her, and dreams that prophesied disasters at places she has never been to.

Acts 2:17-18 tells us that sons and daughters, male and female servants shall prophesy. Prophecy is to speak forth by divine inspiration and/or foretell future events—and many times this happens through dreams. One person commented, "I have found that not everyone believes in prophetic dreams, and even a minister I told seemed skeptical that I have these experiences. I've become selective about whom I tell. I never know the exact meaning of the dreams before I have them.

Acts 2:17-18 tells us that sons and daughters, male and female servants shall prophesy.

Only as events unfold can I piece together the meanings of the communication."

"I simply can't ignore that there is something going on with the dreams. I feel that the majority of people just 'don't get it', or refer to those who have these dreams as 'psychic'. I know that He is the one who has the knowledge and wisdom. I am only a messenger, although I am selective with whom I relate the messages."

"We must have the spiritual gift of prophecy. It was hard at first for me to wrap my mind and spirit around this. Only when these dreams have manifested so many times has my conviction grown iron clad. Now, I find that there is much more I want to learn."

This person was also kind enough to share the dreams she had about national events before they happened:

Some time before 9/11, possibly a couple of weeks, I dreamed that a small plane flew through the entrance of our dining room to our living room. We live in an 1870's farmhouse with double pocket doors. The doors were open wide, but the plane had to tip its wing sideways to pass through. It flew to the other side of the living room and crashed in a ball of fire into our curio cabinet. At that time I passed off the dream as very interesting, but no light bulbs went off. Dumb me, not paying attention to my Heavenly Father!

After the plane crashed into the curio cabinet given to me by my mother, a voice came from outside one of our 4 living room windows, closest to our T.V. cabinet. The voice said this, "There are those who want to see planes fall from the sky." I said in reply, "No! Why would anyone want to see that?!" The message repeated more emphatically, "YES!, there are those who want to see planes fall from the sky!" Then I heard a multitude of people cheering, like they were celebrating something.

"The very morning of this tragic event, I was in our upstairs bathroom when I heard my husband say, "Come quick and watch this on T.V.!" I flew downstairs in time to see the 2nd plane crash into the tower. We were dumbfounded as we watched the chaos unfold live in front of us. It wasn't until some time afterward, possibly months, that I received a 2nd revelation from this dream.

"Our curio cabinet is tall and narrow like a tower, and the window from which the voice came was right by the television. This realization has led me to believe that is why He gives us all this imagery in what seems a mysterious way. He certainly packs a lot of meaning into a short dream! I think the more deeply we meditate upon our dreams, the more we can peel back the layers upon layers of meanings. I am beginning to believe that every detail has significance. Something else I have wondered about - why was the voice coming from outside the window vs. inside the room? I think because it was not from our worldly realm, but from the spiritual realm outside of our own."

This is another prophetic dream she had:

"Before the Gulf Oil spill I had two dreams a short time apart. The first dream took place at night. I was walking near a swampy area with tall grasses at the edge of the water. Even though it was pitch black, I saw an alligator hiding there in the water. It gave me a feeling of menacing evil. In my dream, no one else saw the alligator. Later, I had a dream that I was way above the earth looking down as if from a satellite. I saw the Gulf waters from that altitude.

They were stagnant, and this was the message, "The whole world is concerned."

"That morning I told my husband of the dream. I thought it was strange because we have never been able to travel far from our farm with the animals and crops to look after, and I don't think about geographical areas or look at maps very often. There was no reason for me to think about the Gulf of Mexico.

When the rig exploded and spilled so much oil into the ocean that we wondered if it could ever be contained, I started to look online to see if anyone else had dreams of this. I found one man who saw the rig explode in his dream. I keep asking myself if it was really an accident. I feel that the alligator represented evil that had knowledge of this event beforehand since it was hiding, and the blackness of night represented not only the oil but a deed cloaked in secrecy (an example of why He gives us imagery, to denote more than one meaning). The swamp seemed to represent the stagnation of our ocean and the death of so much sea life. I read that even the currents have been altered. I kept having the feeling that our Creator was very sad that His beautiful ocean had been desecrated in this way."

God Speaking To Us All

After I had completed this book and was in the final stages of the editing process, I decided to read Perry Stone's book *How to Interpret Dreams and Visions*. I was surprised that he included two dreams about national events that were the very same events (9/11 and the Gulf Oil Spill) that I had included in this book. It was a miraculous confirmation of God speaking prophetically to Christians through their dreams.

Perry's dreams were completely different. He dreamed of five tornadoes surrounding the World Trade Center. Each tornado symbolized calamities: 9/11, Iraq War, Hurricane Katrina, 2008 Recession, and the Gulf Oil Spill. These events are "one more step in the economic collapse of America".

In his dream he saw two one-story red brick houses on each side of a 'wall street' that were filled with retired ministers. There was a harvest (being destroyed by the tornadoes) right next to the ministers' homes they were 'retiring' in. The little red brick houses reminded me of the Three Little Pigs story. If it were my dream this would symbolize the generation of pastors in America who looked to their own security and retired on the safe side of Wall Street. Perry in his dream symbolizes a different generation on the other side of the wall in the midst of the storm, sounding the warning and having to take shelter in the Lord, and leading others to take shelter.

"The harvest is plentiful, but the workers are few. Ask the Lord of the harvest, therefore, to send out workers into his harvest field" (Luke 10:2).

Perry Stone shared his World Trade Center dream on television a year before the 9/11 attack. However, the person who had the 9/11 dream in this book had the dream only a couple weeks before it happened, and she didn't understand the dream until after it happened. She commented, "If prophetic dreams were only accepted as truth that God speaks to us in our dreams, and we would pray for increased discernment, then possibly we could prevent tragedies from taking place."

End times prophecy

God give us prophetic dreams as a testimony to who He is. "For the essence of prophecy is to give a clear witness for Jesus" (Rev. 19:10). In the Bible several dreams are recorded at or near the time of Jesus' birth, and near the time He returns (a second time) there will be many more prophetic dreams and visions (see Acts 2:14-21).

"The Book of Daniel is the apocalyptic book of the Hebrew Bible. Its sister book would be the Book of Revelation. And in fact the Book of Revelation is largely a Christian interpretation of the Book of Daniel." "What makes the Book of Daniel different from all other books, is it's built around a series of five dreams, or revelations, that purport to lay out, in step by step fashion, what will actually happen in the last days" (Norman Cohn, Apocalypticism).

In the book of Daniel chapter seven, Daniel has a dream of the distant future where kingdoms rise and fall and God's everlasting kingdom is established. The Daniel Project is a documentary movie that investigates and depicts the various elements of end times prophecy in the Bible—including Daniel's dreams—and how they fit into current events. "The Daniel Project is a genuine investigative documentary that puts ancient predictions under a journalistic microscope... taking the viewer on a journey while presenting only historical facts and observable evidence".

9

Spiritual Warfare

Not only does the Lord declare what is to come through prophetic dreams, He also shows us His plans and the plans of the enemy. James Goll in his book *Dream Language* explains, "Not everything you receive is a declaration of what is supposed to come to pass. It is possible that the Holy Spirit could give you insight into one of Satan's schemes or plans. (Paul said that we are not to be ignorant of the devil's schemes.)" For example, Elisha the prophet constantly frustrated the efforts of the king of Syria. The prophet seemed to know even what was whispered in the Syrian king's bedroom.

> "And the mind of the king of Syria was greatly troubled because of this thing, and he called his servants and said to them, "Will you not show me who of us is for the king of Israel?" And one of his servants said, "None, my lord, O king; but Elisha, the prophet who is in Israel, tells the king of Israel the words that you speak in your bedroom" (2 Kings 6:11-12).

Another example is the prophet Agabus telling the apostle Paul that he would be bound in Jerusalem.

"Coming over to us, he took Paul's belt, tied his own hands and feet with it and said, "The Holy Spirit says, 'In this way the Jewish leaders in Jerusalem will bind the owner of this belt and will hand him over to the Gentiles'" (Acts 21:11).

Spiritual Boot Camp

I worked for the Army for six years, and God used it as a spiritual 'boot camp'. The first three years I was a low ranking part-time computer teacher. I had no real ability to effect change—I had no contact and was far from the powers that be and really didn't understand how the Army worked. God spent this time refining me—which can be seen in some of my dreams in the Prognostic chapter. I depended on the fruit of the Holy Spirit such as patience and long-suffering.

The last three years I worked for the Army I was promoted to a higher ranking full-time position. The Lord placed me in the same building and on the same floor as all the department and division heads, and right across the street from HQ. I began to understand how the Army worked, what the problems were, and some avenues for addressing problems. God spent this time developing my gifts through spiritual warfare—which can be seen in the dreams in this chapter. During this time, I studied over the armor and weapons in the spiritual warfare chapter Ephesians 6:10-20. We are to put on all of the armor of God, stand firm in all things, be alert for attacks, constantly pray, and speak boldly the truth of Christ.

Flaming Darts Dream

I'm at work, and there is a pool downstairs with people in it, and I kind of want to go down there. Someone who reminds me of an old boss in Hawaii is my boss's boss, but maybe higher up (region or HQ). She takes me upstairs to talk about my performance. It appears that she has something bad to say. I'm ready to listen, but she never really says anything concrete. Then we are still upstairs but below her office, and she has a bunch of women laying and standing around her. A couple of them are only wearing some straps, and their posteriors and other parts are exposed. I tell her we're not going to talk as long as all these women are around.

Then, I'm downstairs on the main floor (not downstairs where the pool is), and there is a dark-skinned tough guy who says he's here to bounce me out of here (my workplace). I tell him that if he touches me I will report it to the police because that is assault. I think we both know that if he has other assault charges against him already that could land him in prison. He doesn't do anything and is walking downstairs. I tell him I am going upstairs to talk to her again, and he can take me out after that.

Then, she comes through the front door of the main floor with a bow and arrow and is going to shoot me. She shoots an arrow? As I run out the back door I hear her telling that guy she has 200 arrows and has a special sight (mounted on the bow) for accuracy. I go out one set of doors then another and then check my inner sense if I should hide to the right of the door, but I don't think I should.

Then, I'm running through a field/garden as fast as I can and trying to follow the leading of the Lord and staying to the right where she might not be able to see me. Then I take a left on two paths that are

to the right hoping she can't shoot me in the back and wondering if
that guy is helping her.

I had this dream the last year I worked for the Army. The setting was work and the pool was a symbol of emotion. It was the draw of getting emotionally caught up in all the drama at work with the *"people who were already in it"*. It is the way down (*downstairs*) and not the way up. My boss's boss in Alaska had transferred in from the Hawaii region office and was symbolized by the woman in my dream who was an old boss in Hawaii. I had previously addressed with this lady the false accusations my boss had made on my performance review where *"she never really says anything concrete"*.

Most of the leadership and employees were women. The women *"below her office"* was a symbol of being under her chain of command. It was a toxic organization (e.g. gossiping, vindictiveness, cronyism, etc.). It was the her job to do something about it, and until she did I wasn't willing to negotiate (*"I tell her we're not going to talk as long as all these women are around"*).

I had confronted my boss up the chain of command about her character assassination, intimidation, and bullying tactics (*"tough guy who says he's here to bounce me out of here"*). The Lord showed me through this dream that I was right in addressing the sins of gossip, slander, cronyism, bullying, etc, in the workplace. We are to be a light in the workplace and not remain silent. We have a responsibility to stand up for the truth and against sin.

"Do not participate in the unfruitful deeds of darkness, but instead even expose them;" (Eph. 5:11).

In the last part of the dream, I'm getting ready to address more issues up the chain of command (*upstairs*), but *"she comes through the front door of the main floor with a bow and arrow and is going to shoot me"*. The 200 arrows were the data entry and correction (that wasn't a part of my job) that they dumped on me shortly after this dream. They handed me a stack of excel spreadsheets with the fixes, and I was amazed at the Lord when the line count came out to right at 200. The *"special sight for accuracy"* was them demanding all the fixes be double checked for accuracy.

I objected but complied and completed the assignment. They told me they were going to turn the task over to the people responsible for this work. However, a few months later they dumped it on me again. I was weary after years of battle and I evaded doing the work (*"running through a field/garden as fast as I can...hoping she can't shoot me in the back"*). One Bible commentary points out that in the chapter on spiritual warfare (Ephesians 6) there is no armor for the back, "nothing to defend those who turn back in the Christian warfare." Was God telling me through this dream, stop running and stand up against the attack or stand in faith and patiently endure?

In my dream and in real life I kept checking for the Holy Spirit's leading. Looking back now I realize I needed to look in the Bible and discern His will. He showed me this scripture: "If a soldier demands that you carry his gear for a mile, carry it two miles" (Matthew 5:41). I complied the first time but I didn't second time (i.e. carry it the second mile). God promises not to give us more than we can handle.

"In all circumstances take up the shield of faith, with which you can extinguish all the flaming darts of the evil one" (Eph. 6:16).

Spiritual Attack Dream

"For we do not wrestle against flesh and blood, but against the rulers, against the authorities, against the cosmic powers over this present darkness, against the spiritual forces of evil in the heavenly places" (Ephesians 6:12).

This passage talks about powers of darkness and evil spiritual forces, and Ephesians 6:11 also talks about the schemes of the devil. I usually look at all of these evil powers as the enemies' team—and not in particular whether it's the devil or an evil spirit or whatever. We are in a spiritual battle not a physical one, but the enemy does make physical attacks like in the following dream that someone shared.

"The old barn with its massive, hand hewn, oak beams and wooden pegs still stood. Last spring we decided to have this old barn taken down before it fell down. I wanted to save the timbers and siding, so we hired a man and his two helpers to dismantle it in a way that would not destroy the lumber. It was shortly before this that I had the unusual dream that I was near a construction site. The message in the dream was this: "Run straight, not sideways." I found myself thinking, "Don't worry Mom, I'll be careful." My mother was always a worrier and told us repeatedly to "Be careful."

It was a windy spring day when the men were dismantling the barn. I asked my husband to go with me so I could take a look at their progress, and I also wanted to see where they had piled the siding that I wanted to save. When we arrived, there was nothing left of the barn but a shell. All the tin had been removed from the roof, and the siding was gone also. The huge timbers could be seen quite easily now. I had to walk around the barn to get a look at the large pile of siding near the creek. Being cautious by nature, I stayed some distance from the structure as I made my way around it.

Suddenly, I heard a loud CREAK from above! Without looking back, I started to run back toward our vehicle away from the barn. At one time, I could run like a streak of lighting, but it had been years since I ran like that. As the entire barn collapsed behind me, I kept running without looking back. I just made it to safety before the heavy beams hit the ground. My husband said they missed me by 5 or 6 feet! My heart was pounding so hard that I wondered if it would ever return to normal.

> *I recalled my dream and the message, "Run straight, not sideways."*

Later that evening I recalled my dream and the message, "Run straight, not sideways." Now, it finally made sense! If I had run straight out from the barn as it fell, instead of parallel to it, I could easily have gotten out of harm's way. Oh, when will I learn to listen to every word that He gives me, and pray for increased discernment!

The next day, I decided to return to the site. The men had taken the backhoe and knocked the rest of the barn down since the previous day's incident had rattled all of us. I wanted to look for square nails, hinges, or any other antique pieces of hardware from the barn. I did not want to give in to fear over what had taken place the day before.

A friend of my husband's was on a tractor in our field, applying anhydrous ammonia which is used to improve crop yields. My personal opinion is that it is too dangerous to justify the benefits. Many farmers have had hoses break and been sprayed with ammonia. The tractor was in the distance when we arrived.

I found myself caught up in the moment, bent over looking for nails and not realizing that this man was getting closer and closer with the tractor and applicator. Suddenly, I was engulfed in the ammonia which had drifted my way! My husband was further off in the field, talking on his cell phone and didn't notice what was happening. Before we left the house I felt that I needed to take my jacket, even though it was not cold that day. I jumped into the truck, but the windows were down and the ammonia drifted in. I grabbed the jacket that I brought along and covered my face with it as I jumped back out and ran further away in the field. I sank to the ground, safe at last, but wondering if I had breathed in this horrible stuff and damaged my lungs. Luckily, I was alright. I have always hated the smell of ammonia and never use it in the house."

Spiritual Battlefield

John Wesley wrote in his journal that there were people in several cities that threw rocks at him and tried to attack him when he came to preach. Years later the people in these towns miraculously welcomed him. Anyone who is advancing the kingdom is bound to be targeted by the enemy, and it seems the bigger the advance the more intense the spiritual warfare.

When I was working for the Army it was constant spiritual warfare, but there were two weeks in particular that were insane. It was a time of excruciating endurance as I stood up for what was right regarding the technical aspects of a building project I was involved in.

The first week was a spiritual battle through the bosses emailing up several levels of the chain of command about the project. The following week was email exchanges with the contracting and public works departments and the government contractor who was doing the building project.

I was ready to call in sick after they scheduled a meeting with me and the contractor and those two departments (that were making things difficult). Yet, God seemed to tell me in my dream it would be okay. "Fear not for I am with you" (Isaiah 41:10).

I dreamed I was swimming in the ocean in Hawaii and it was very shallow, and I was speaking some Hawaiian lingo as I backstroked and sort of felt like I was impressing the locals a little. The water got way too shallow so I had to turn around, and then I got to a deeper area but not over my head. There was a naked old guy swimming with his rear end facing me. I tried to ignore him as I continued to enjoy my swim. Underwater it was so clear, and I could see for a distance. I was amazed that it could be so clear without goggles.

Then I was on shore looking for my wife, worried about her, and went to look for her at a dormitory that had two pairs of split diagonal stairs going up. She wasn't there so I went out, and a girl who liked me had parked my bike next to hers. I grabbed my bike from behind hers and drove off fast to try to find my wife at the hotel next door. She wasn't in the lobby, and I thought about looking at the register on the counter to see if she had signed in. I was worried about her.

This was a prophetic dream. It was simply God showing me the things to come. The feelings in the dream were good, and I wasn't sure how this dream correlated with the meeting I had that day, but I hoped that it was a promise that it would be so shallow (versus over my head) that I would even have to turn back. And sure enough, I faithfully arrived at the meeting, but the bad guys (the two departments who were causing problems) never showed up.

> You shall seek those who contend with you,
>   but you shall not find them; (Isaiah 41:12)

I praised the Lord! I looked around, but the enemy was nowhere to be found!! I was redeemed! The meeting was the VERY opposite of being in over my head. It was like my dream, where I was comfortably swimming along (doing an easy backstroke) in shallow water, and everything was amazingly clear (like the water in my dream).

The contractors weren't like the contracting department portrayed them. I had come into the meeting ready to compromise and forget about standing up for what was right, but I didn't have to compromise, and we quickly came to an agreement as we chatted about the construction project. I even came out looking like a hero because I took care of something right on the spot that was holding up the project. The Hawaiian lingo in my dream was me speaking a little construction lingo with the contractors.

I had thought earlier that maybe the dream also had something to do with the gym because that was the only place I saw naked old guys. Lo and behold, after the meeting I went straight to the gym, and after my workout as I walk in the locker room there was a naked old guy with his rear end facing me. I laughed to myself and thought God really does have a sense of humor. He could have used any symbol for the gym, but He used the one that I find very unappealing about the locker room.

After the gym, I went home for lunch. At this point, after seeing the first two parts of my dream fulfilled, I expected that my wife would be somewhere else (like in my dream) and she was! She is usually home for lunch, but I realized it was Friday. She had to pick up our kids from school earlier on Fridays.

I was worried about her (like in my dream) after all this spiritual warfare from work that had been taking a toll on my family. She arrived thirty minutes later, and I shared with her what had happened! The Lord had been showing me all week in various ways a theme of redemption—and then on the last day of the work week He redeemed me!

In Isaiah, God challenged the Israelite's gods to do the things that He does.

> Let them bring them, and tell us
>> what is to happen.
> Tell us the former things, what they are,
>> that we may consider them,
> that we may know their outcome;
>> or declare to us the things to come.
> Tell us what is to come hereafter,
>> that we may know that you are gods;
> do good, or do harm,
>> that we may be dismayed and terrified.

(Isaiah 41:22-23 ESV)

Going Before Me

When things don't feel right, or I'm confused and there is conflict or more than the usual hindrances, I stop and try to discern if what is really going on is spiritual warfare. If it's spiritual warfare, I try to not get caught up in it, but instead step back from what I'm doing, close my eyes, patiently pray, and preserve my energy until it passes.

I've noticed that God speaks to me through my dreams more frequently when I am in times of hardship, transition or turmoil. God put Joseph, the husband of Mary, through the hardship of marrying a woman pregnant with a baby that wasn't his, and after Jesus was born he had to flee in order to protect Him. God gave to Joseph four dreams surrounding the birth of Jesus (in the first two chapters of Matthew). God guided Joseph through his dreams, telling him where to go, when to return to Israel, and warned him not to go up Judea.

In September of 2013, I had the following dream:

There is a group of ladies that are going to rent my red Toyota Corolla (our car in real life). I was uncomfortable with the deal, kind of like I didn't know what I was getting into.

I'm in a mechanic's garage, and the Corolla is up on the lift. A mechanic tells me that I could have gotten a better deal renting out the car. He said the ladies are paying $350 for work on the car (in exchange for the rental of it) but renting it is worth $899.

I go into a hallway in the garage, and there is this large heavyset guy who is the mechanic, and he can't work (on the car?) because of his back. It's like he is really worn out from working, and his back is giving out on him. He goes back to lying down in a metal trough of sorts that is V-shaped inside.

It looks like the work on my car will be delayed, so I still have some time to change the deal. I go outside and want to find the ladies to call the deal off or renegotiate because it's not worth it, but they're far off or not there.

I had applied for a special two-month developmental assignment in the Army Public Affairs office (PAO), and I had this dream the morning of my first day working for them. My wife and I had prayed a couple times before this dream for a good desk and office during this temporary assignment, for favor from my co-workers, and that the Lord would go before me. The Lord answered my prayers by telling me, through this dream, the circumstances of this temporary work assignment.

The car symbolized me. I have had many car dreams, but this may be the first where it was actually my car in real life. This assignment was tapping my real talents as a writer. The PAO was constantly in need of content, and I was there to write news stories for the newspaper. The PAO got me as a 'rental' for two months without having to pay any salary and with very little work on their part (*"the ladies are paying $350 for work on the car (in exchange for the rental of it) but renting it is worth $899"*).

When I arrived the first day, I met with the PA officer lady, that morning she had slipped on the new ice on the sidewalk and was going to leave to get her back checked because she had back problems (*"his back is giving out on him. He goes back to lying down"*). She was kind of heavyset—just like the mechanic who was having back problems in my dream.

This was the first time I had met her, so there was no way I could have known any of this! During my assignment she decided it was time to retire and ended up retiring a couple months after my assignment ended (*"he is really worn out from working"*). After I had started my assignment I had to go back to my regular job for awhile when civil service workers were furloughed due to a government shutdown over the budget (*"the work on my car will be delayed"*).

The first mechanic in the dream could very well have been an angel of the Lord telling me what to do. I felt the Lord was telling me through this dream that I had some bargaining power. I asked for a desk in a private office, like I had prayed for, and they gave it to me. There were two other ladies in the office that were under the PA officer and oversaw my position. The second day of my Public Affairs assignment I had to confront both of those ladies on their micromanaging behavior.

It was a toxic work situation, not unlike the department I already worked for, but I had the confirmation and courage through this dream to stand up for what was right throughout the assignment. I had to face some angry attacks, but I kept my cool and stood my ground—just as the Lord tells us many times 'to stand' in the Ephesians passage on spiritual warfare. The fruit of this assignment was that I was able to publish in the Army newspaper a two-part article on the widespread problem of toxic leadership in the Army.

10

Japan Mission Dream

In 2010, I had a dream where I was at Denny's restaurant with my wife, and we were seated across from a white guy. It appeared that he spoke Japanese and had some Japanese business customers with him. The name of his business is something like Japan Go. I seem to remember considering a job position with that company in the past.

The second part of the dream the restaurant turned into a train in Japan. This man and the Japanese people just got off on the previous train stop. I had a very strong feeling that we (myself and my wife and kids) should have followed them and gotten off on that stop. Two stops later my wife thinks we should get off the train, and I follow. We cross over the tracks, and I regretfully realize that I left my green luggage bag on the train. The train is riding off, and my wife takes a picture of the back of it (with the train number) so that we can try to locate our bag later.

The first part of this dream was no surprise, it was a very literal image of our afternoon activities for that day. Neil Verwey from Japan Mission (http://japanmission.org/) was giving a sermon in Japanese at my wife's Japanese Bible study. When I was living in Japan I frequently ate at Denny's restaurant. Food is a symbol of spiritual nourishment and restaurants a symbol of nourishment in a public setting, i.e. the Bible study.

The *"Japanese business customers"* were the people in this study who financially supported his mission work. The business name *"Japan Go"* is symbolic both of the Japan Mission organization and the call to be a missionary in Japan. I heard him speak the previous year at the same Bible study and at that time felt a strong desire to be a missionary abroad (*"considering a job position with that company in the past"*).

The second part of the dream was a sort of warning that I was going to miss an opportunity symbolized by that train stop. My wife had to leave early to pick up our kids from school, and I was going to leave at the same time. However, my sense from the train portion of my dream was that I was to stay with the Japanese group, i.e. the Bible study, so I stayed another hour.

I told Neil that my wife has a heart for Japanese coming to Christ and that her family is Buddhist. He suggested that Japan Mission could send their newsletter, Yorokobi no Izumi, to her family without our name on it. I came home and told my wife about it, and she said a couple days ago she had prayed for God to send her family someone or something to help bring them to Christ (not including herself). She realized this was the answer to her prayer. It was a difficult decision to make because she feared her family's reaction, but she decided to have Japan Mission send their newsletter.

The luggage bag symbolized something that has been weighing us down—her family's salvation—and losing the bag symbolized a chance that we could lose and would have to try to regain. My wife taking a photo is her trying to later recapture this chance for reaching her family.

Neil also talked about God using his faults or weaknesses in real life, such as being forgetful. One time he got off at the wrong train station, so he asked God who or what was the reason for getting off here. Then he met someone and shared about Jesus.

After getting to work that day (after talking with Neil) I realized I was also supposed to be at work earlier because the kids at the youth center got out early on Wednesdays. This was the only time I have ever been late to work, but somehow God had made me forgetful even in the face of my wife leaving to pick up our kids (who also get out early on Wednesdays)! The Lord made me forgetful so I would stay later and talk with Neil and not miss out on a chance to evangelize our family in Japan!

Neil was surprised to hear that I dream a lot and said that he doesn't dream very much. He also shared the following dream with me (which I quote from an article he wrote).

HEAVENLY PANCAKES

"So many are wondering how I am doing emotionally since Peggy went to her heavenly abode on 5 December, 2008! Well, Saturday night, 20th of December, 2008, I read what Peggy was writing to us who are left behind, about suffering – and it was as if she was writing to me personally!

It is not God's intention that you should look down at the grave or down into the emptiness of your breaking heart, but rather to look up into the face of God and see there His love and purpose for your life. Never allow God's work to suffer while you feel sorry for yourself, but put your grief into new energy for service. There are too many around us who are also suffering and in need of our help.

These words of comfort still freshly in my mind triggered a strange dream when I dropped off to sleep. In my dream, Peggy and I were still very young, fair, and energetic. We invited 2 very special people over for a brunch, and we wanted to give them the very best we could afford. We had a tin of Lyle's Golden syrup stashed away for a very special occasion. Some of you might be old enough to remember the famous golden syrup of that time. It was a mouth-watering delicacy, especially for children! The tin was a deep green, bearing a picture of the rotting carcass of a lion with a swarm of bees, and the slogan, 'out of the strong came forth sweetness'. This is a reference to chapter 14 of the Book of Judges in which Samson was traveling to the land of the Philistines in search of a wife. During the journey, he killed a lion, and when he passed the same spot on his return, he noticed that a swarm of bees had formed a honeycomb in the carcass. Samson later turned this into a riddle at a wedding: Out of the eater came forth meat, and out of the strong came forth sweetness.

In my dream, Peggy and I served our distinguished guests pancakes with the special golden syrup. Well, one of our guests had already eaten a hearty breakfast before he turned up, and holding his tummy, he did not want a single bite of our specially prepared pancakes. The other guest enjoyed them just as much as Samson enjoyed his honey and could not stop talking about the wonderful brunch we prepared. Suddenly, in my dream the guests and Peggy disappeared, and I was completely alone and so sad that tears welled up in my eyes! I was staring at the pancakes and the opened tin of golden syrup and feeling very, very sorry for myself! Unexpectedly, there was a clamorous noise at the door! People wanted to come in, and I still had plenty of pancakes and golden syrup to serve them!

As I woke up, I was lingering in bed thinking about the meaning of the dream, and then I knew that I still needed to serve heavenly pancakes and the golden syrup to many hungry people! Some would be so engorged with what the world gives them that they would not like my heavenly pancakes, but some of them will be hungry for them!

Jesus took the five loaves, and looking up to heaven, He blessed and broke and gave the loaves to the disciples; and the disciples gave to the multitudes. (Matthew 14:19,20).

A little crumb from Jesus' table can satisfy for all eternity! (Matthew 15:27)."

Flying, Planes and Trains

An encouraging dream for me can be one where I am flying or about to take off in an airplane or in a train station about to depart in a positive direction. I had many flying dreams after I surrendered my life to Christ—dreams where I felt so good having the ability to fly through the air. The flying part means I am soaring high spiritually. In one dream I am very confident of my flying ability and have no worries about falling or losing my flying power—which is about my relationship with God and my assurance of salvation.

I have also had train dreams that were symbols of me being stuck on a set course of action. In my previous dream, on the train in Japan, it showed that I needed to change a set course of action; in this case, we changed our plans for the day. In the Bible Abimelech was given a warning dream, and he changed his course of action:

"But God came to Abimelech in a dream by night and said to him, "Behold, you are a dead man because of the woman whom you have taken, for she is a man's wife." Now Abimelech had not approached her. So he said, "Lord, will you kill an innocent people? Did he not himself say to me, 'She is my sister'? And she herself said, 'He is my brother.' In the integrity of my heart and the innocence of my hands I have done this." Then God said to him in the dream, "Yes, I know that you have done this in the integrity of your heart, and it was I who kept you from sinning against me. Therefore I did not let you touch her. Now then, return the man's wife, for he is a prophet, so that he will pray for you, and you shall live. But if you do not return her, know that you shall surely die, you and all who are yours" (Genesis 20:3).

Sometimes, it's a course of action that can't be changed. One morning I had a dream where I was on a train and sad that my wife wasn't with me when I needed her. That day, my wife had already committed to do something else with my son, and it wouldn't be fair to change the plan just as they were headed out the door. If I would have listened to the leading in my dream earlier we would not have had gotten set in an unchangeable plan (symbolized by me stuck alone on a train in my dream).

Mexican Dish Dream

I was in a restaurant with my wife and kids and my mother, her husband and my brothers. There was a wait to be seated. We went into the back room and let the kids start eating pasta with red sauce (off the buffet or something). They were eating it at some area where there were trays where dirty dishes are put on (since we didn't have a table yet. However, there were several open tables in this room.

I came back to tell everyone that the wait was going to be really longer than we thought. They all agreed that we should go somewhere else. I went to tell the wait staff. The waitress was bringing out my order, and it was a delicious Mexican meal that I hadn't tried before. She sat down to be friendly with me, and I pointed out my wife and parents waiting at the front of the restaurant.

I figured I would eat this plate since they had already made it, and it looked so delicious. I got my napkin on the top of it and pulled it off and looked to see if there was paper on top of my food. It came with a small, round, white cheese (crumbly type?), and they handed me a *small dish with a sort of dipping sauce or salsa. I wasn't interested in the sauce but politely took it. I thought I might try the white cheese with the dish since it appeared that it was supposed to be eaten together. Then they unwrapped it somehow and I woke as I was about to take my first bite.*

I was going along with the crowd in my dream that didn't want to wait, but just as I was ready to tell the wait staff we were leaving they brought out a delicious looking Mexican dish that I didn't know and wanted to try. I had already submitted this book to the printer and to Kindle online. I thought I was done and was just doing some last minutes edits. The morning of this dream, I woke up early and worked on a piece I had just added to the spiritual warfare chapter. I found that all of a sudden I was reworking the whole chapter and modifying a couple other chapters.

The Lord wasn't finished with the book—kind of like when the Lord told Neil Verwey after his wife's passing he still had delicious Heavenly Pancakes to serve to the hungry. This was spiritual food from the Lord—and Mexican is my favorite!

I discovered the "small, round, white, crumbly cheese" was Queso Fresco. This fresh cheese is fresh insight in my writing. This cheese is made by compressing the water (editing and cutting words) out of curds, and with more compression the cheese becomes crumbly (every word carries weight).

Putting sauce or salsa on is about giving the book some mass appeal which *"I wasn't interested in"*. There was more to be revealed (*"then they unwrapped it"*), something good, new and unexpected. The Lord answered some questions I had and gave me new revelation and clarity into dreams I already had in the book.

11

Answers in Genesis Dream

On May 5th, 2010, I had an astrophysics and nuclear engineering dream. This dream was an example of how we can try to translate our dreams, using dream dictionaries and other means, and come up with an interpretation that is completely different than what God had intended. In my case, a couple weeks later the Lord revealed what the dream was really about. Here is the dream:

I had a dream where I'm with my son and daughter at CSU (where I used to work) in something like the engineering building. I am trying to find a way out of the building. We go down some stairs and over a metal ladder that is quite a tight squeeze to get over. I see signs for an emergency shampoo bath for those who get chemicals on them in the rooms below. We had already gone out this way once before, but this time I didn't want to have my kids go down in that area near those rooms because of the danger of chemicals. The way back over the ladder is even smaller than before, and I don't think I can get through. I talk to someone on the other side, and they try to tell me how to get through.

Next thing I know I'm downstairs with my kids (we ended up going there after all). There are some people, and one is a guy talking about how he was an astrophysicist but got into nuclear engineering because he took a chance and applied for a highly competitive scholarship that he thought he would never get.

Here was my first interpretation of this dream:

I believe God was telling me through this dream that I'm already on the narrow way, (that is following Jesus) and that I just have to proceed forward and release my fears (claustrophobic feeling of wanting to get out) and worries about myself and my kids. I have to go the way down, because the way up is down. The way to live in Christ is to die to self. The way to be lifted up by Christ is to humble ourselves.

Here are some scriptures on humbling ourselves:

"Do nothing from rivalry or conceit, but in humility count others more significant than yourselves" (Philippians 2:3).

"The LORD lifts up the humble; he casts the wicked to the ground" (Psalm 147:6).

"Humble yourselves, therefore, under the mighty hand of God so that at the proper time he may exalt you" (1 Peter 5:6).

"Humility comes before honor" (Proverbs 15:33, 18:12).

Here are some dream dictionary symbol definitions from online websites:

"Astrophysics - a branch of astronomy dealing esp. with the behavior, physical properties, and dynamic processes of celestial objects and phenomena.

Nuclear - of relating to the atomic nucleus -reaction -physics, used in or produced in a nuclear reaction -fuel -waste -energy.

Nucleus - the central and most important part of an object, movement, or group, forming the basis for its activity and growth.

Engineering - the application of science or mathematics by which the properties of matter and the sources of energy are made useful to people."

Astrophysics and nuclear engineering seem similar to the layman like me—highly scientific and mathematical, but after looking at the definitions I can see the difference and how it applies to my life. God, like the nucleus, is the central and most important part of everything and is the basis for all our activity and growth. Engineering is the application of God's Word by which His power is made useful to all people. Astrophysics is the study of the behavior, properties, and processes of celestial objects. Celestial objects are a symbol for God.

I could probably spend more time unpacking all the symbols in the dream, but I think I've gotten the general gist of what He's trying to say to me. I believe He is telling me I will move from focusing on understanding the character of God and the processes He has gone through with man (the history in the Bible) to the application of His power here on earth in all kinds of situations (kind of like the way we can use nuclear energy for different purposes). It will require me to take chances on something I think is impossible but ultimately is possible for God (e.g. applying for a job I think I have no chance of getting).

The "Revelation"

On May 5th, 2010, I had the previous dream, and I spent some time looking into the meaning of the dream and wrote the above interpretation about it, but it didn't hit me until May 23rd that this dream was actually about the class we started attending on the evening of May 6th.

I had been praying for a way to teach our kids more about the Lord, and there was a flyer at church for a class to teach kids about Genesis. I thought this was an answer to my prayer—and it was—but what God was showing me through this dream was that this class would have just as big an impact on me as it would our kids. The class introduced us to Answers in Genesis (AiG), and to say that class rocked my preconceptions about creation, the solar system, and the dinosaurs is a gross understatement. AiG is nothing other than God's own divine truth revealed. I was in the middle of reading the whole Bible for the third time, but that class took God's Word to a whole new level for me. It showed me the deception that the secular world had brainwashed us with and showed me how God's creation really happened.

The biggest impact for me was about dinosaurs. It's so obvious in the Bible that they are the Leviathan, the Behemoth, and dragons. "Job 41 describes a great animal that lived in the sea, Leviathan, that even breathed fire. This 'dragon' may have been something like the mighty 55 foot long Kronosaurus, or the 82-foot long Liopleurodon" (Ken Ham, What Really Happened to the Dinosaurs?).

"Take a look at Behemoth, which I made, just as I made you. It eats grass like an ox. See its powerful loins and the muscles of its belly. Its tail is as strong as a cedar. The sinews of its thighs are knit tightly together. Its bones are tubes of bronze. Its limbs are bars of iron. It is a prime example of God's handiwork, and only its Creator can threaten it. The mountains offer it their best food, where all the wild animals play. It lies under the lotus plants, hidden by the reeds in the marsh. The lotus plants give it shade among the willows beside the stream. It is not disturbed by the raging river, not concerned when the swelling Jordan rushes around it. No one can catch it off guard or put a ring in its nose and lead it away" (Job 40:15-19-24).

Some Bibles say the Behemoth is an elephant, hippo, or mythical creature. However, you can certainly catch and lead an elephant, and I'm sure that God wouldn't be talking to Job about a mythical creature, so only dinosaur fits the description. Lastly, dragons are mentioned in the books of Job, Psalms, Isaiah, and Revelation. Considering the legends of dragons throughout the world's cultures, it makes sense that these dragons are what we today call dinosaurs. In addition to the other evidence presented by AiG, I have no problem now believing that the dinosaurs were created on the sixth day with all the other animals and thus are only

6,000 years old and became extinct like so many other plants and animals in this fallen world we live in.

Why did it take until May 23rd (eighteen days after my dream) for me to understand what my dream was about? I didn't read all the packets they had given us in the class until after I was intrigued by the third week's session on dinosaurs. Then the dream meaning became clear to me as I was reading the packet about the solar system. There was an article from a Ph.D. Astrophysicist (from my home state of Colorado) who explained the fallacy behind the big bang theory: "Despite claims to the contrary, we've never seen a star forming. Star formation seems to be nothing more than a secular attempt to explain the universe without invoking God" (Dr. Jason Lisle, The Stars of Heaven Confirm Biblical Creation). That is when it clicked with my astrophysics dream. How often do I have anything to do with, or read anything about astrophysics in my life? Never!

One question I raised during a couple sessions of the class was about carbon dating. One AiG theory is that carbon could have been different before the flood. I didn't realize that carbon dating is just used for living things, and radioisotope dating is used to determine the age of rocks. In my mind (and probably in many others) this carbon/radioisotope dating was key to my belief about the millions of years of creation.

"The world is awash with evolutionary propaganda centered on dinosaurs. This has resulted in the thinking of even Christians being permeated by evolutionary philosophy" (Ken Ham, What Really Happened to the Dinosaurs?). The problem with 'historical' science is that we really can't tell how things age over many years—it's just guesswork and theories that are presumed to be fact. "All radioisotope dating methods assume (among other things) that the decay rate of a given isotope (an atomic nucleus with a given number of neutrons) is constant—that it has always been what it is today. The RATE researchers have uncovered several independent lines of evidence that strongly indicate that nuclear decay was much more rapid in the past" (Dr. Jason Lisle). (This astrophysicist explaining nuclear decay was symbolized by the astrophysicist unexpectedly became a nuclear engineer in my dream.)

Here are my own thoughts about decay: Adam lived 930 years, and Noah lived 950 years. After Noah, each generation had successively decreasing life spans. This was a fulfillment of God's Word (Genesis 6:1-3) to make man's life span 120 years (after the flood). Decay began with the first sin, but it sped up after God's pronouncement to decrease man's life span and His judgment with the flood. And today the average life expectancy has fallen much lower than 120 years. "The years of our life are seventy, or even by reason of strength eighty" (Psalm 90:10). If God can radically change the decay of man, how can we make any assumptions about nuclear decay over six millenniums?

In my dream I was trying to protect my kids and find a safe way out from the engineering building (at CSU the physics department was also in that building). This class was *"someone on the other side trying to tell me how to get through"*. Instead of escaping the area I was trying to avoid in my dream we ended up there. As Christians we must speak the truth about the fallacy that's at the core of evolution "science". Ken Ham states, "A non-Christian is not neutral. The Bible makes this very clear: 'The one who is not with Me is against Me, and the one who does not gather with Me scatters' (Matthew 12:30)." Evolutionary science scatters theories around presuming to be fact and ends up deceiving children, adults, non-Christians and Christians alike.

"Down through the ages, people such as the Egyptians have worshiped the sun. God warned the Israelites, in Deuteronomy 4:19, not to worship the sun as the pagan cultures around them did. They were commanded to worship the God who made the sun—not the sun that was made by God. Evolutionary theories (the 'big bang' hypothesis for instance) state that the sun came before the earth, and that the sun's energy on the Earth eventually gave rise to life. Just as in pagan beliefs, the sun is, in a sense, given credit for the wonder of creation" (Ken Ham, Six Days or Millions of Years).

I don't consider myself a man of science—I find it very interesting, but I don't base my beliefs on it. I take God's Word as truth based on the miracles He has done in my life, but God wanted to show me His glory even deeper. He gave me the scientific explanations even when I wasn't asking for them. He gave them to me on a level that I could understand and even explain to my kids. This is how my prayer to teach my kids about Him was answered. This was the part of my dream symbolized by the *"highly competitive scholarship that he thought he would never get".*

I believe God gave me this dream to confirm the truth that He was about to reveal to me and the effect it would have on me. I had no clue what He was about to show me through a class I thought was for my kids. I had thought after I finished reading the Bible for the third time that God was going to take me deeper into Revelation, but He took me the exact opposite direction. Instead of to the end of time, He showed me the beginning of creation.

I've written many, many interpretations of my dreams, and sometimes mistakes are made when we try to hear God whether it's through our dreams or any other kind of leading. My Answers in Genesis dream is a good example of God's faithfulness to show me the correct interpretation.

I've mainly tried to include dreams in this book that had real life confirmation that my interpretation was correct. Interpretations of my other dreams have served to guide me and are cause for reflection, but many times the confirmation was simply in my own heart. This Answers in Genesis dream had an undeniable real life confirmation.

12

Career Dreams

M y career dream is to make a living writing books, and I often pray that the Lord bless my book business, but in the meantime, I, like many artists, have to make a living to support my dream. Recently, I sold my Takamine guitar to a guy who had just become the worship leader at a church here on the island. He said he had to support his music by working as a carpenter. I've spent the last twenty years doing teaching and IT jobs to support my family. I've continued to write off and on, and ten years ago I published my first book.

In my journey to make a living and provide for my family, the Lord has given me several job related dreams. I've included in this book three different dreams that occurred before three different job interviews: a computer teacher job in 2008 (in this chapter), an IT job in Alaska in 2011 (see the chapter on Prophetic Dreams), and a historian job in 2014 (in this chapter).

The Lord will surely reveal and confirm what He is about to do in your life. For the first two interviews (in 2008 and 2011) I got the job. I'm still waiting to hear back from the last one. It's on hold because of budget issues (just like the 2011 job).

I've also had three dreams about three different jobs I felt He was telling me I shouldn't pursue, and I've included those dreams at the end of this chapter.

Teaching Job Interview Dream

In May of 2008, I had a dream of going swimming at the ocean at the hotel. I was walking around with only a towel and my privates were showing, and I didn't care even though people were looking.

Next I'm captured by some bad guys in the basement of a hospital? I outsmart the guy watching us and get him to let us use his passcard to access the computer and phone.

I had already had one interview with the boss, and the day I had this dream I was going in for a second interview with the boss's boss who was a local Japanese lady. From this dream I knew that I needed to watch my ego symbolized by the way I was walking around exposed and not caring if other people saw. I went into the interview knowing I should watch my ego with the local lady in the interview (a common problem between local Asians and mainland whites).

The really amazing part of this prophecy was the fact that the boss, who had interviewed me before, gave me a heads up while I was in the waiting room that many of the questions would be the same, so I had a chance to think them over again (*"guy watching us...let us use his passcard"*).

In my dream I'm trying to get out, but in my interview I'm trying to get in. The guy in my dream wasn't one of the people keeping me from escaping but seemed to know what was going on. The boss guided me in the interview to be a success by nodding and just letting me know I was on the right track. It was like my dream where we got the guy's passcard and swiped it on the computer, and I swear he saw me swipe it but pretended not to notice.

The setting of this dream was a time of transition (between jobs) symbolized by the hotel. Some time after I got the job, I had a dream that my workplace was a hospital just like in this dream—kind of a foreshadowing of what was to come. In that dream the hospital was a symbol of God working on me through this difficult workplace (*"some bad guys in the basement of a hospital"*).

Job Application Dream

I'm finishing school and taking an exam in a classroom with others. The behavior questions are easier to figure out but not the science ones. I spend five minutes on the third question (skipped the first two) which seems to have several approaches to it, but I'm starting to get the idea and I think I have the answer, so maybe the rest of the test will flow easier now that I have figured out the way the questions work. I have only an hour total or a minute per question.

Next I'm in an office with a couple guys who have a job for me. They say something about Jesus people, but I don't say anything. They say I can get the exam to them later. I say Monday, but they say end of today which is Friday. They are basically letting me cheat because I could also look up all the answers and take as much time as I want?

I'm in my locker or room, thinking how to make time to do the exam today and not skip the rest of my classes which are also last day parties. My next class is 5th period, and it's some math class. I haven't attended the class all semester and don't know what will happen. I'll have to skip it to do this test but don't want to miss the last day parties either? I will have to do the exam (like I would have done in the class anyway) without looking up anything and get it done in an hour, because I don't have the time to do it any other way.

I'm trying to do the exam, and a couple of girl classmates are there. One is leaving, and I don't say anything because I'm focused on the exam. She makes an effort to say goodbye to me, so I say goodbye back to her.

In the middle of May, before our move back to Hawaii while still in Alaska, I had applied for a Cultural Historian job in Hawaii. The job fit my college degree, and I had written a couple books on culture. I only sent my cover letter and resume and didn't bother filling out the state government application because I thought it was a waste of time, and I really didn't think I had a shot at getting the job.

On June 4th, I received an email stating that they couldn't send me a letter because I had only put the city and no address on my application. In addition, no position was mentioned so no further action would be taken. I had put the city of my intended residence in Hawaii on my application without an address because we were still in Alaska. I replied the next day that it was for the Cultural Historian position and asked if I would still be considered.

I had this dream on Wednesday, June 11th, and we had just moved into our apartment. On Friday, June 13th, I received a response to fill out an attached state government application, and it would be sent to the department for their consideration. I was surprised I was even being considered for this job and wanted to reply the same day, Friday, but our internet wouldn't be connected until Monday ("*I say Monday, but they say end of today which is Friday*").

In my dream I was focused on the exam but thought I should say goodbye to a girl classmate. I was also wondering in real life if I should email this lady back and tell her I couldn't get the application back to her right away. I finally emailed her on Monday that I would mail her the signed application, and she replied okay.

In the dream I felt it was almost cheating. The deadline had already passed for the job application, but they were kind and still let me submit the government application after the fact. At this point, I started thinking it was God's hand doing the impossible. If they had just sent a letter through the mail I wouldn't have had the ability to email back and ask if I was still under consideration. The fact that they replied and were still considering me after the deadline was a miracle.

In the last part of my dream, I was trying to figure out how to juggle everything. I had other things we were working on like trying to buy a used car as soon as possible, since we were paying for a rental car. We were spending the weekends looking at used cars. The weekend was symbolized by the end year class parties in my dream.

Historian Job Interview Dream

In 2014, I had a dream I was at work. Several ladies and everyone is playing some kind of memory game. Each time it comes to me, I seem to have forgotten what it was the others had said before me. It was like a one word answer. It seems others were doing the same and just going to the next thing without remembering and then laughing together as I try to remember myself what it was that the previous

had said. I ask them and they tell me. Then I ask something more
serious, and they are working on answering my question.

Later in the dream I think I was watching a music video, and now
I'm actually there. Two guitarists are sitting on a stage and just
finished a song. I'm walking along. The dark haired guitarist on the
left is cool and crosses his leg. I can see he is wearing some boots.
They are soft boots with soft soles kind of like a mukluk that was
trendy awhile back. It was kind of like watching an old video seeing
old styles.

The whole dream had a really friendly feeling, like feeling part of the group, and people were being nice when others didn't have the answer like me.

This dream was about a job interview I had the next day with a really nice guy who had a list of questions—and many of them historical preservation terminology that I didn't know—but he was nice about it and sort of led me to figuring out the answers. There was also one point where I was trying to remember what he said. The interview very much matched up with the first part of my dream, and I was thinking this as it was happening in the interview.

The last part of the dream was about the last interview question which was 'what do you think is the most important thing to preserve in Hawaiian culture?' I told him the language and suggested that they offer Hawaiian language in high schools in conjunction with the performing arts. He said that was a good idea and that performing artists had been one of the major elements of keeping the Hawaiian language alive.

Showing Me What's in My Heart

I had three dreams about three different jobs I felt He was telling me I shouldn't pursue. The first week I was in Japan on Christmas vacation, I was thinking how good the guy, who has the same job I had in Alaska, has it there in Japan. I believe the Lord gave me the following dream to show me my heart and that I really didn't want his job.

1st Dream:

I was in the region office of one of the higher ups that I know, and he was telling me how the highest paid of them is a guy named so and so, and he makes $26 an hour (I think it might also be 56k a year?).

Then I'm with some lady from the region office and another lady that's one of my peers in HR. The lady from the region office is giving me a performance review and telling me I got a B grade. And I was thinking at least it wasn't a B minus—that would have been bad.

She said there was problem that according to the rules I had to cut my hair. I told her that she could see in the manual a picture of me with short hair (with kids). She said that didn't count because I was with kids. I was thinking I should have got it cut the previous week because I had been thinking about doing it. They said I had until two o'clock to give them an answer. I told them I need to check the legal regulations and to give me 24 hours or until tomorrow.

The B grade symbolized the excellent, but not outstanding, performance reviews that I had gotten in the past working for this department. The neither plus nor minus grade is neither negative nor positive feedback from them.

Getting a haircut is a symbol for changing your mind. The Lord was showing me that if I worked for the Army again they would be legalistic and try to force me to change my mind through the bullying tactics they used before, and once again I would be fighting legalities and searching employee handbooks to clarify rules.

2nd Dream:

For several months I had been thinking of applying for a teaching job at a local Christian school. My last week of vacation in Japan, I was thinking that I would have to apply for that teaching job when I got back to the USA, and then I had this dream:

I was attending high school and was very popular at first, but then I was writing notes on someone's cell phone with a mechanical pencil and scratched the screen. I felt bad and promised to find something to get the scratch out.

I'm in a study group for a history class, and some high school guy says he is going to the junior high dance. I tell him I used to go to that school. Then the history study group people leave because I haven't studied and don't know my history.

I'm driving home thinking I really have to do my history studies. There is a car having trouble in front of me and pulls alongside another car that is helping it. They both have their lights off. Mine are on and so are most of the cars up ahead.

The Lord was telling me through this dream that if I taught computers, I'm not up on the latest technology, like mobile, and would only screw it up. If I taught history I would soon lose their confidence and start thinking it would be easier for me to teach junior high kids instead of high school.

The last part is symbolic of the fact that employees are required to be Christian. There will be those whose lights are shining and some that aren't, and some are even breaking down.

3rd Dream:

A week later, at the beginning of January 2015, I had this dream:

I'm desiring a younger than me blond girl, and she wants to rent a small red sports car. I think this will help me win her. We're at a rental place that she knows, and I sit in the tight little red sports car. It's not an awesome new style but a kind of cheaper older style, but it's a still a red sports car. The lady in the rental office is faced in my direction, and I'm worried she will figure out my intentions with the blond girl.

The rental lady comes over with the blond girl and starts explaining the rental car and agreement. She says something about wanting us to return it by 5 am on Dec. 24th. I didn't realize it was so close to Christmas and was thinking the date would be the 23rd. That date is going to be a problem. Apparently I have a brown haired girlfriend, and she might find out about me and the blond. I was also thinking that I wanted to sleep in, so we would have to find a way to return it later.

The rental lady, an older blond, goes over to a sort of metal cage and continues explaining. I say yes I understand the piston system and she says it's not the pistons. I look more closely and see that she is right. She continues explaining it. Apparently it is something we're supposed to know as part of the rental.

This dream is not about lust but about potentially being unfaithful to God's plan. Many men struggle with sexual thoughts (and that is why pornography is such a problem—even in the church). However, in the writings of the prophets in the Bible, adultery and sexual impropriety are used as symbols of unfaithfulness to God.

That day, I got an email that my application was updated for a job in Japan, and when I looked at the status I saw that my application for a foreign service IT job had been referred for additional consideration. The blond in my dream symbolizes my desire for this Foreign Service job, but the Lord is telling me that I am desiring something that is unfaithful to God's plan.

I really desired that blond in my dream and was willing to get the red sports car rental to get her. The sports car rental symbolizes the Microsoft certification I would have to attain (and pay for) to get the job. I'm confident I can get the certification, but that doesn't guarantee me the job. In the dream, I know I can get the rental car but that doesn't guarantee me the girl. The last part of the dream is telling me that I think I know everything needed for the certification, but there are things I don't know symbolized by the lady telling me it's not what I think, and that it won't be anything I'm interested in—which it isn't.

The Lord is telling me that it's closer to Christmas than I realize which could symbolize spiritual gifts. In writing this book, I am using the spiritual gifts of faith (inspiring others' faith through my example) and prophecy (speaking the truth). This dream also came a couple months before publishing this book. One person commented, "I think that this book will be the "Christmas gift" in your dream and will result in many blessings for you."

13

Dream Conversations

In the Bible, a great part of Daniel's witness to non-believers was through dreams. Daniel interpreted Nebuchadnezzar's dreams and "made it extremely clear that the dreams and the handwriting would not, could not, be revealed through his own power, but only explained through God's wisdom and power which would disclose the dream to Daniel."

I had a co-worker who was part of a cult called the Black Israelites that believes only blacks are saved. I had been talking to him extensively about the Bible and contrasting what he believed with the Bible. Later on he told me he had a dream where he was beating up someone. I explained to him that was a symbol of him beating up the part of himself that person represented.

Later, it hit me that he was talking about me in his dream. It was obvious that the Lord was trying to tell my co-worker something through his dream—yet he refused to understand. He was, in essence, fighting against the very truth that was being spoken to him and was being confirmed in his heart through his dreams.

> *A great part of Daniel's witness to non-believers was through dreams.*

In the Bible, even non-believers saw clearly the meaning of someone else's dream:

"Gideon crept up just as a man was telling his companion about a dream. The man said, "I had this dream, and in my dream a loaf of barley bread came tumbling down into the Midianite camp. It hit a tent, turned it over, and knocked it flat!" His companion answered, "Your dream can mean only one thing—God has given Gideon son of Joash, the Israelite, victory over Midian and all its allies!" (Judges 7:13-14).

"Barley grain had only half the value of wheat, and the bread made from it was considered inferior" (Life Application Study Bible). God put this symbol in the dream because barley bread symbolized inferiority to the Midianite man having the dream. Gideon's army was 300 men against 15,000, so in the eyes of a Midianite it would certainly seem inferior. The Midianite's dream was evidence of how God speaks through our dreams—to both believer and non-believer—and gives us symbols that we can understand.

Dream Dialogue

The following is a great dream conversation I had with someone I know (and quoted with her permission). You can see how the Lord is using both repetition and later revelation.

I've had people ask me what their dream means, but it's really the Lord who reveals the meaning. I try offering suggestions for symbols in the dream and even how I might interpret the dream if it were my own dream. However, as you can see from this conversation, only the Lord can reveal the meaning in His own way and timing. Many times we can try to interpret the dream, but the actual interpretation comes down to waiting on the Lord to see if He will reveal further details. (This is one of the lessons I learned from my earlier Answers in Genesis dream.)

Anon: It's been months of the same dream every night that I'm failing high school math and P.E. I'm not only done with high school, but I'm done with college. I haven't taken a math or P.E. class in 8 years.

Brent: If it were my dream I would pray that the Lord reveal to me its meaning. In my life a failed math class might mean something isn't adding up right in my life, and the P.E. class would have something to do with health I suppose. I believe God gives reoccurring dreams because He has something He wants to tell us, but we're not hearing it.

Anon: Yes, whatever this message is it must be important, because it keeps getting louder!

I spent a lot of time contemplating that dream today, and I think it is because I have been exploring several different careers that would mean doing up to two years of undergrad work before I could change professions or begin a graduate program. I feel very disheartened at the thought of being back at square one, so to speak. Math and P.E. were my least favorite subjects, so I think that's where those specific subjects chime in.

Brent: Sounds like you're on track for understanding your dream.

A year later

Anon: Remember my trapped in school dreams I wrote you about?? I analyzed and analyzed these dreams. The message only seemed to get more deafening, until I was having some sort of dream every night where I was back in junior high or high school trying to explain to people that I'd already done this, this wasn't where I was supposed to be, this was inappropriate, etc. Between you and I, literally the day that my boyfriend and I broke up, the dreams stopped. Pretty interesting!

Brent: Junior high and high school sounds like having to deal with immature situations. Failing the math class might mean having to deal with a thinking type person/situation as a feeling type and not succeeding. The Lord will show us the meaning and the way as we seek Him.

Anon: Wow, I LOVE that insight about the immaturity! I had an amazing Apocalypse dream a few nights ago that was so intense I was awake for hours with my heart pounding (I think it had to be so intense so that I woke up and remembered it). All week I keep finding more and more meaning in it!!! It was an amazing dream. It definitely was just personally relevant to me though, not a literal disaster coming .

Brent: Apocalypse is the beginning of God's reign and the end of the age.

Anon: Well, that's what the dream was about! It was about finding root in something deeper than worldly stability. Some of the symbolism was really easy to figure out (we were hiding from the horrific storm in a church that had a super strong foundation that went deep into the earth).

Our leader was a guy that was a "survival expert." But he kept leading us astray with bad judgment calls. I woke up after we had barely outraced a tornado and barely made it back to the church. I asked him, "Are you grateful we made it back?" And he said, "No, the lucky ones die."

Then he said we were not safe in the church and directed the group to leave. I had completely lost faith in his judgment at this point, and my parents and I decided to stay without the group. I think the man symbolized certain aspects of secular culture that claim to be true but ultimately lead you astray. It was a really intense dream with insane storms and people killing each other for supplies and what not. I think that showed the impermanence of society and the fragility of the world. Everything crumbled so quickly. I remember staring at some money and checks I hadn't cashed yet and thinking that money—the thing that used to rule the world—is now a useless joke.

Brent: Ultimately the Lord gives all meaning. If it were my dream, the guy would be a part of me that is keeping me out of the church and out of safety in real life. A really intense dream means something really intense is going on in my life. The crumbling so quickly reminds me that I cannot rely on people or anything in life or worldly values (such as money) that God is my ultimate source of love, peace, and security.

Anon: Oh, interesting perspective that the guy would be part of me. You are so insightful! I've been trying to find a church community that I connect with—have been "shopping", haha.

Brent: I'll be praying that you connect with a church that's right for you and the one that God wants you to be in! End of conversation.

This apocalypse dream is also a great example in how the Lord leads us to Himself. I had another dream conversation with a close Christian friend. He told me that his business was sort of in a holding pattern. He had a dream he was on vacation. In his dream it was like high school or something where they were picking people for teams and the feelings of whether you're going to get picked or not. It appeared to me that the vacation symbolized his holding pattern with his business, and the getting picked part was about getting contracts for his business. He said he had a lot of proposals out right now, so that sounded like what the dream was about.

It really is amazing how the Lord can show us the meaning of our dream by discussing it with another Christian. Unfortunately, not many Christians in America—including pastors—are interested in listening to God speak to them through their dreams despite the overwhelming evidence in the Bible that God does use our dreams to speak to us.

14
Why Me?

I used to have dreams and wonder if they were just literal events that might happen. Ten years ago, I studied some books on Jungian interpretation of dreams and started to understand how symbols work. About eight years ago I completely surrendered my life to Christ and soon after read Riffel's book *Dream Interpretation a Biblical Understanding*. Later, I had the privilege to exchange email and talk with Riffel on the phone (before he passed away in 2009 at the age of 93). He had decades of experience with dreams and tons of insight.

Over the course of many years, it has been a gradual and increasing awakening for me to hear the Lord speak through my dreams. One person commented, "I have been aware of my prophetic dreams for at least 40 years, but it seems that the more I believe, the more I receive...I believe that the frequency and significance of my dreams and leadings has increased over time to the extent that I cannot deny or gloss over them."

"Not all of my dreams have been extraordinary. Some have been rather mundane, at least from another person's perspective. One morning I told my husband that I dreamed one of our roosters killed another rooster. I asked him to check when he let the chickens out to free range. He came back inside and said he didn't see a dead rooster. I asked him to go outside and check again. He then came back inside and said that he had found a dead rooster that had signs of being killed in a fight."

"What is to be made of this? The only thing I can think is that our Heavenly Father is concerned about each and every detail of our lives, and He knows us down to the smallest details. He knows that I am fond of our animals, and He was telling me this just to let me know that He is present and that He cares.

"I keep wondering, "Why me? Why is our Heavenly Father showing ME these things?" Perhaps because I am willing to listen and know that He is who He says that He is. I accept without doubt. I also wonder who else is receiving prophetic dreams; what percent of our population is He communicating with in this way, and how many do receive these communications but ignore them? Also, can we pray to receive the meaning of our dreams to prevent or alter events, or are they just to gain insight into something after it happens?"

"I don't consider myself a modern day 'prophet' and do not engage in public speaking of any kind nor promote my religious beliefs. I am only a farm wife who sometimes has dreams and leadings of things that come to pass. I could spend a life-time trying to analyze the whole thing, and another life-time trying to answer, "Why me?" I prefer to pray for discernment and try to be a good 'listener' by faith alone, no proof needed."

I also have the same questions, and the first thing that comes to mind is Joseph and his interpretation of the Pharaoh's dream that avoided the disaster of famine for seven years. Maybe there will come a time when He does give us the meaning beforehand so that we can avert disaster. On the other hand, my wife says that it's not to avert some disaster, but to continue to develop our ear in listening to Him. It's God's demonstration that He cares about even the smallest details of our lives.

She also commented, "I think that your wife has correctly discerned that He wants us to learn to listen to Him. I think He could be training us, just as parents train a child to listen... to avert danger or hardships, or just to have a close, caring relationship." She also commented, "I keep wondering if He could be preparing us for something else....?"

Postface: the American Church

According to the Pew Forum, the United States is 79.5% Christian (Global Christianity: Report on the Size and Distribution of the World's Christian Population 2011). Anyone can look in their neighborhood or workplace and see that isn't the case. One Korean pastor of a church in the U.S. grew up in Korea during a time when Christians were persecuted, and he estimates the true number of Christians in the U.S. is probably around twenty percent.

Surveys show that 40% of Americans claim to go to church regularly, but in truth only 20% attend regularly. In the last office I worked, there were nineteen people: four evangelicals (including myself), a non-practicing Lutheran, a Catholic, a Mormon, a guy who said he believed but didn't go to church, and eleven non-believers. I don't know how many (out of the nineteen) would claim to be Christian on a census or a survey; however, only twenty-one percent (the four evangelicals) regularly attended church. We are a nation of goats who think they are sheep (i.e. followers of Christ).

"My sheep listen to my voice; I know them, and they follow me" (John 10:27).

My wife and I spent three years attending a Pentecostal church in Hawaii. I was astounded and in wonder at their ability to ignore scripture and their lack of desire to study and understand scripture. I also asked the pastors if I could start a dream group, and they said they didn't want people going in a bunch of different directions.

In Alaska, we attended a Baptist church for three years only to find they weren't interested in the prophetic. This is where I got my first experience with cessationists without actually knowing it. The problem was they weren't outspoken about being cessationist. It was almost like it was bit of a secret, and I let them dismiss it as an area of differing opinions.

Around that time, I took a class on the Apostle Paul at a Christian university as part of my Biblical Studies certificate. In this class I learned the term cessationism. The textbook, like the Baptists (and the Evangelical Free church), taught cessationism without actually calling it that. Relegated to the very end of the text book was a discourse on how the spiritual gifts were historical and ended after the first apostles. In class we debated what the coming of 'the perfect' (1 Cor. 13:10) meant, and there were quite a few students (possibly more than half) who believed the spiritual gifts had ended.

After we returned to Hawaii, we attended an Evangelical Free church. As I began to write my book on dream interpretation, I shared that fact with people in church and Bible study and found out they also believed like the Baptists. They were also hesitant to discuss it and said there are many interpretations, positions and opinions. Again I was astounded and in wonder, just as I was with the Pentecostal church, at their ability to ignore what scripture said in light of the fact that they appeared to be serious about studying scripture.

One person commented, "There will always be those who will doubt unless they themselves have had a personal experience of something. I would be arrogant if I thought that I had the power within myself, completely without God, to know beforehand that something was going to happen. I consider myself only the receiver or messenger of whatever He is showing me. Even though I usually can't discern at the time what is the meaning of each dream, there most certainly is a meaning and message that He wants me to know."

Through many scriptures and personal accounts I have shown that God truly does still speak to those who have ears to listen. I encourage everyone to keep a dream journal and pray for discernment about their dreams. Now are all these leadings and dreams just figments of my imagination? I'm not saying I understand them all perfectly. Sometimes I wonder, but there are times that the pieces fit together and speak straight to my heart and situation, and I know that it can only be a Divine Creator setting things in motion and showing me what is to come.

Acknowledgments

A very special thanks to Mary Spahr who made many contributions through dreams, comments, and editing.

I would like to say a big thank you to all those who contributed to this book. Above all, sincere praise and gratitude to the Lord Jesus Christ for bringing me this far, and His inspiration and insight in my writing. He's Alive!

About the Author

Brent Massey is an Christian author and publisher. He has read the complete Bible several times and has a Certificate of Biblical Studies from Colorado Christian University. He lives in Hawaii and is also the author of *Culture Shock! Hawaii*, *Where in the World Do I Belong??*, and *Discovering the Water of Life*. He can be contacted at brentmassey@brentmassey.com and is interested in hearing from people from around the world.

www.ingramcontent.com/pod-product-compliance
Lightning Source LLC
Chambersburg PA
CBHW020038040426
42331CB00030B/15